"Bryant Wright has done a remarkable job jolting faithful believers into the realization that *The Stage Is Set* for the end times. Don't just read this book. Pass it on!"

Michael Youssef, PhD, author of *Jesus, Jihad, and Peace*

"This book is a clear and concise study of the end times. It is both biblical and relevant to the world in which we live. One need not agree with all the details of interpretation to benefit from its insights. The future is bright because Jesus is coming again. This work will get you ready for that glorious day."

Daniel L. Akin, president of Southeastern Baptist Theological Seminary

"Insightful. Hopeful. Needed. In a world that seems to be crumbling around us, *The Stage Is Set* reminds us that God paints on a canvas bigger than we can see or imagine. If you have ever questioned what will happen when Jesus returns, this book is for you!"

Louie Giglio, director of the Passion Movement; author of *The Comeback*

"Bryant Wright has accomplished what too few pastors today even attempt. He has addressed the pressing questions of the eschaton that church people deeply desire to have their pastor answer, and he has demonstrated that his grasp of the Scriptures provides preparation for the last days. *The Stage Is Set* provides a priceless evaluation of the false promises of the pseudoprophets of the era and instructs the church in constructing a godly response of witness and life in the gradually darkening theater of this age. Do not miss this pastor's insights into the last days."

Paige Patterson, president of Southwestern Baptist Theological Seminary

"To show how much I respect, admire, and believe in Bryant as a teacher and expositor of God's Word, I am endorsing a book on eschatology from the perspective of a premillennialist, while I myself am a pretty stubborn amillennialist. Having said this, if you want to be well-informed and encouraged from all perspectives, *The Stage Is Set* is a must-read book. Bryant is in a rare class of those who handle well God's Word."

Randy Pope, founding pastor of Perimeter Church

"Bryant Wright, writing about his beliefs concerning the end times, has courageously stepped into waters that many have previously. Obviously, some will not agree with everything he says, but unlike many books on this subject, *The Stage Is Set* is irenic not polemic, direct but not dogmatic, substantive but not speculative. It belongs on the bookshelf of all who are interested in the last days, and we all should be!"

James Merritt, lead pastor of Cross Pointe Church

"Bryant Wright delivers the truth from God's Word regarding future events and the second coming of Jesus. I highly recommend this insightful and inspiring book. The message of *The Stage is Set* will prepare you for life and eternity."

Dr. Jack Graham, pastor of Prestonwood
Baptist Church

"I am blessed as I read Dr. Bryant Wright's book, reminding me of our blessed hope. Jesus's return inspires and instructs my life in holy living and how to urgently share the gospel."

Dr. Johnny Hunt, senior pastor of First Baptist Church;
former president of the Southern Baptist Convention

"The intensity level of any competition rises greatly as the clock winds down. Players become more determined. Each gives an all-out effort. Every move matters. In *The Stage Is Set*, my friend Bryant Wright looks at today's news and headlines through the lens of Old and New Testament prophecy and concludes that the end of the age is near. Believers should not fear this conclusion. Instead, it should drive our efforts in missions and evangelism. We must make every moment count until our Lord's return."

Kevin Ezell, president of the North American Mission Board of the Southern Baptist Convention

"We all know it is coming. We can sense it in our bones and read it in the news. This world is heading somewhere and seemingly fast. More than political pundits, we need biblical theologians to guide us through the confusion and into the compelling nature of the end times. In Bryant Wright's latest book, *The Stage Is Set*, you will gain a watchful eye and biblical heart of understanding of what our eternal future holds. Don't miss the outstanding message in this book."

Gregg Matte, pastor of Houston's First Baptist Church; author of *Unstoppable Gospel*

"Many Christians are at a loss when it comes to understanding what the Bible says about the end times. This area of study, called eschatology, is often muddied with a number of differing opinions. What Bryant Wright's voice offers to this discussion is clarity and trustworthiness. *The Stage Is Set* draws its information from two sources: careful biblical exposition and years of walking through the biblical landscape described in end-times prophecy. Ultimately, this book reminds us of the urgency and need to finish Christ's work of making disciples who make disciple-makers."

Robby Gallaty, pastor of Long Hollow Baptist Church; author of *Growing Up* and *Rediscovering Discipleship*

"Over the years of hosting *100 Huntley Street*, I have interviewed hundreds of people. They come from different backgrounds, with different goals, but they have one concern that is common among most Christians: What is going on in the world? Bryant Wright has written a compelling book that answers this question in a thorough yet easy to understand examination of biblical prophecies and Revelation. When you read the news of the day, you'd best have this book beside you."

> **John Hull,** lead pastor of Eastside Baptist Church;
> host of *100 Huntley Street*

"This book is both brave and biblical. It reads current events in the light of the Scriptures, not the other way around. Most of all, it encourages Christians and unbelievers alike to be ready for the final act in the drama of redemption—the return of Jesus Christ."

> **Timothy George,** founding dean of Beeson
> Divinity School of Samford University;
> general editor of the *Reformation
> Commentary on Scripture*

"Many books, most of them driven by world events, deal with the topic of the end times and Christ's return and victory. In *The Stage Is Set*, Dr. Wright shows from Scripture, both the Old and New Testaments, how we have been living in the last days for two thousand years. This book is clear, fair, and easy to read. I highly recommend it!"

> **Matt Carter,** pastor of preaching and vision
> at The Austin Stone Community Church

THE
STAGE
IS SET

ISRAEL, THE END TIMES,
AND CHRIST'S ULTIMATE VICTORY

BRYANT WRIGHT

BakerBooks

a division of Baker Publishing Group
Grand Rapids, Michigan

Published by Baker Books
a division of Baker Publishing Group
P.O. Box 6287, Grand Rapids, MI 49516-6287
www.bakerbooks.com

Printed in the United States of America

Library of Congress Cataloging-in-Publication Data
Names: Wright, Bryant, author.
Title: The stage is set : Israel, the end times, and Christ's ultimate victory / Bryant Wright.
Description: Grand Rapids : Baker Books, 2017. | Includes bibliographical references.
Identifiers: LCCN 2016033233 | ISBN 9780801019517 (pbk.)
Subjects: LCSH: End of the world—Biblical teaching. | Eschatology—Biblical teaching. | Bible—Prophecies. | Bible—Prophecies—End of the world. | Providence and government of God—Biblical teaching.
Classification: LCC BS649.E63 W75 2017 | DDC 236/.9—dc23
LC record available at https://lccn.loc.gov/2016033233

Scripture quotations are from the New American Standard Bible®, copyright © 1960, 1962, 1963, 1968, 1971, 1972, 1973, 1975, 1977, 1995 by The Lockman Foundation. Used by permission. (www .Lockman.org)

17 18 19 20 21 22 23   7 6 5 4 3 2 1

To the people who have been with us
on our sixteen Bible study tours of Israel,
where biblical prophecy comes alive.

To Carrie,

Hope in Christ,

[signature]

Contents

Introduction

That We Are Living in the End Times Is Indisputable

As a pastor, I am continually asked, "Do you think we are living in the end times?"

"Absolutely," I answer, "it is indisputable." Yet current events are not the main reason. What may surprise you is how long we have been in the end times. When Peter stood to preach on the very first day of the church at Pentecost, he explained what was happening through the lens of Scripture. He quotes the prophet Joel (Joel 2:28) when he writes, "'AND IT SHALL BE IN THE LAST DAYS,' God says, 'THAT I WILL POUR FORTH OF MY SPIRIT ON ALL MANKIND'" (Acts 2:17). God's Word is clear. We are living in the last days. The end times are here!

In that light, Peter's sermon at Pentecost serves as a great model. It has a blend of Old and New Testament prophecy that explains why we are living in the last days. That will be central to this book. Studying the biblical prophecies of the Old and New Testaments together gives the complete

11

picture of where our world is headed and why I believe we are living in the end times of "the last days."

Scripture is very clear: the world is headed toward a time when all hell will break loose on the face of the earth, especially against Israel. Anti-Semitism is on the rise like no other time since before World War II. Islamic regimes and ideologies fuel this rise. With the increase in the number of Muslims in Europe, fear of offending Muslims causes the most secular regimes of the world to reek of anti-Semitism, for secular people often turn their backs on supporting Israel to appease Muslims riddled with anti-Semitism.

Nationalism is on the rise in places like China and Russia. More and more business has the feel of a global village—one world, one expanding economy. A growing unease in feeling things are out of control and falling into chaos is making everyone wonder about the future.

When the worldwide economic bubble finally bursts, the world will seem to be falling into hopeless despair. There is no question: the stage is set.

It is sobering. It can be frightening. But followers of Jesus have great hope! Even in the midst of our increasingly evil and chaotic world, we live with the hope of Christ's coming again. When He does, He will come to judge evil. But that's not all. It will mean salvation for Israel in more ways than one. It will usher in a new age in which His kingdom will come, and His will be done on earth as it presently is in heaven. At last, life on earth will be as we long for it to be! It will be glorious.

Yet the most important question is this: Will you be included in the celebration of this new age? Or will you be left out? I hope to help you to see what Scripture reveals, and I pray it will help you prepare for the future.

1

Birth Pangs

The Signs of the End of the End

In early January 2016, the Chinese stock market sent shudders throughout the financial world. The Dow on Wall Street saw its sharpest one-week drop in all of history. Everyone wondered, *Where are we headed? What's going to happen?*

By now, that is ancient history. Yet it is one of thousands of reminders that everyone is interested in the future, particularly with regard to the economy. *How will it affect my job, my investments, my retirement?* We live in a 24/7 news cycle when it comes to the economy, and when the market has a dramatic drop, people tend to panic and worry. They ask, *What does the future hold?*

Those of us who have lived for a while contemplate the future for our kids and grandkids. *What will they do? What will they become? What kind of world will they have to navigate?* The potential is unlimited, but the dangers are frightening.

In 2014, the press bombarded us with a deep-seated fear of the Ebola virus. *Could this become a plague that infects and kills millions?* Yet by the time you read this, the crisis will have been largely contained. The Ebola scene that absolutely dominated the news is now long gone from the news cycle. By early 2016, Zika was another new virus to become the world's concern. Every day it seemed a new crisis became the focus of our attention. They caused us to ask then what we ask now—*What does the future hold?*

Islamic terrorism stunned our world on 9/11. Today it is a daily concern—not only in the Middle East but also here in the United States. Outside threats keep Americans on edge. ISIS stays on the move either in gobbling up territory or being in retreat. Vladimir Putin seems determined to restore Russia to the status of being the United States' top competitor on the world stage. Then there is China, which seems poised and determined to replace the United States as the number one world power. What adds to this fear is most Americans' unease at the thought that the United States is losing its grip on world leadership. Donald Trump went a long way pouncing on that fear.

We are all interested in the future, and Jesus's disciples were no different. In the last week of Jesus's ministry, they were sitting with Him on the Mount of Olives, looking at Jerusalem. Centered in their sights was the temple of the Jews that had been dramatically renovated under King Herod the Great. It was an awesome sight. Nothing in their world could compare to its majesty. Some of the boulders in the giant wall around the temple weighed more than two hundred tons. The columns on the Temple Mount were breathtaking. It was built to last.

Yet what Jesus told them must have stunned them: "Do you not see all these things? Truly I say to you, not one stone here will be left upon another, which will not be torn down" (Matt. 24:2).

They were absolutely dumbfounded. How could it be? It was inconceivable to them. It would be like you and me standing on the Jersey shore in the spring of 2001, looking out across the Hudson Bay at Manhattan and a religious leader we respect saying, "See those twin towers of the World Trade Center? They will be completely demolished. Not one stone will be left standing." That would have been inconceivable to us then. And yet the inconceivable occurred the morning of September 11, 2001.

What Jesus said stunned His disciples. They responded like we would, "Tell us. When will all this happen? What sign will signal your return and the end of the world?" They were just like us. They were interested in what was going to happen in the future.

Jesus's prophecy about the destruction of the temple would be fulfilled about forty years later when Rome completely destroyed the temple in AD 70. Not many of the disciples would live to see that day, but Jesus did answer their question by speaking of the signs of the times.

Sign #1: Many False Messiahs Will Come

And Jesus answered and said to them, "See to it that no one misleads you. For many will come in My name, saying, 'I am the Christ,' and will mislead many." (Matt. 24:4–5)

False messiahs are not new. A great example of one occurred in AD 135, a time when persecuted Jews were desperately looking for a messiah to rid their promised land of the
deeply resented Romans. Rome had totally demoralized the
Jews with the destruction of their temple in AD 70.

Amazingly, in AD 118, when Hadrian had become the
emperor of Rome, he was sympathetic to the Jews. He allowed some of the Jews who had been expelled from Israel
to return to their homeland and even granted permission
for the rebuilding of the temple. But then he went back on
his word and began deporting Jews to North Africa.[1] Rome
had taken them through one disillusionment after another.

Sadly, by AD 132 Hadrian began to build a temple to the
Roman god Jupiter on the site of the Temple Mount where
Rome had destroyed the Jewish temple. This understandably
led to a huge Jewish rebellion. This revolt was led by Shimon
Bar-Kokhba. He began to be seen as the Jewish messiah to
save the Jews from the yoke of Roman rule. Speculation of
him as the Messiah was heightened because the Bible refers
to the Messiah as a "star," and Kokhba means "star."[2] But
even more important, he was a descendant of King David,
which the Bible says clearly the Messiah would be:

> When your days are complete and you lie down with your
> fathers, I will raise up your descendant after you, who will
> come forth from you, and I will establish his kingdom. He
> shall build a house for My name, and I will establish the
> throne of his kingdom forever. I will be a father to him and
> he will be a son to Me; when he commits iniquity, I will cor-
> rect him with the rod of men and the strokes of the sons of
> men, but My lovingkindness shall not depart from him, as
> I took it away from Saul, whom I removed from before you.

Your house and your kingdom shall endure before Me forever;
your throne shall be established forever. (2 Sam. 7:12–16)

For a time, Shimon Bar-Kokhba led the Jews to many
victories over Rome, but the might of Rome was too great
and by AD 135 the revolt was crushed. At this point all Jews
were expelled from their land, and Israel was no more. To
add insult to the Jews, Rome renamed their Judean land
Syria Palestina. Palestina was the Latin derivative of the ancient Jewish enemies, the Philistines. Thus, for almost two
thousand years the land was known as Palestine. It was not
until May 1948 that the nation of Israel was reborn, and not
until the Six-Day War in 1967 that Jerusalem and the Temple
Mount were again part of Israel—a key miracle that is central to much prophecy of the end times being fulfilled. But
Shimon Bar-Kokhba would be one of many false messiahs to
appear on the world scene. In every age, Jewish moms-to-be
would speculate if their son to be born was the long-awaited
Jewish Messiah.

In the twentieth century, especially with the rebirth of
Israel, the number of false messiahs skyrocketed.

Many Jews around Brooklyn began to speculate that
Rabbi Menachem Mendel Schneerson, who was the last
Lubavitcher Rebbe, could be the Messiah. I remember standing at the western wall in Jerusalem in the early 1990s and
seeing Jewish banners that read, "The Messiah is coming."
The Rebbe never claimed to be the Messiah, but amazingly,
after he died in 1994, many Orthodox Jews expected him to
rise again. Even when he didn't, some still believed he was
the Messiah.[3]

Yet what is so interesting is that many who claimed to
be the Messiah in the last fifty years were not even Jewish.

The second half of the twentieth century saw a rise of false messiahs.

Jim Jones, the pastor of the People's Temple in Redwood Valley, California, became famous for his followers "drinking the Kool-Aid" (they were told to drink Kool-Aid that had been poisoned with cyanide) in a mass suicide in the jungles of Guyana on November 18, 1978. Like so many false messiahs, he instilled in his followers the vision of establishing a utopia here on earth—with himself as the all-powerful unifier and leader.[4] I was in seminary when the world heard the news of the mass suicide of his cult. It terrified me to think a religious leader could have that kind of influence in people's lives. Yet all false messiahs are evil, if not this obviously.

In 1993, **David Koresh** was the leader of the Branch Davidians cult outside of Waco, Texas. Born Vernon Howell, he changed his name to David Koresh, which is a Hebrew transliteration of Cyrus, the Persian king who allowed the Jews held captive in Babylon to return to Israel. He convinced the followers in his cult that he was the modern-day head of the biblical House of David, which is essential for the biblical Messiah.[5] He followed a long line of false messiahs that led many of their followers to self-destruction. He died on April 19, 1993, at the cult's compound after a fifty-one-day standoff with federal agents.[6]

Sun Myung Moon, whose followers were known for selling flowers on street corners and holding mass weddings of up to two thousand couples at a time, is probably the most famous self-proclaimed messiah of the twentieth century. His followers were known as Moonies. He was born in what is now North Korea and settled in the United States in 1972. At a banquet in March 2004, which included hoodwinked members of Congress at the Dirksen Senate Office Building in Washington, DC, he shocked the attendees by saying that emperors, kings, and presidents had "declared to all heaven and earth that Reverend Sun Myung Moon is none other than humanity's savior, messiah, returning lord and true parent."[7] He died in September 2012 at the age of 92. He's still dead, along with a long line of false messiahs.

That's a character trait of all false messiahs. When they die, they stay dead. Eventually, their movements die with them. Obviously, Jesus is very different. He predicted not only that He would be executed but also that He would rise from the dead on the third day (Matt. 16:21; 17:22–23; 27:62–28:15). And He did.

It is amazing that despite the huge number of false messiahs and self-destructive cult leaders of the twentieth century who mislead so many, there appears to be even more in the early days of the twenty-first century.

In Japan, **Mitsuo Matayoshi** is a political figure who has called for a world economic cooperative. He, of course, would be the leader and sees himself as "the only God Mitsuo Matayoshi Jesus Christ."[8]

In Brazil, **Inri Christo** is a classic false messiah who fits the stereotype of so many false messiahs—a religious man who wants to justify having many women around himself. He sees himself as the reincarnation of Jesus.[9]

In the Philippines, **Apollo Quiboloy** claims to be the appointed son of God and is the founder of an organization he calls "The Kingdom of Jesus Christ, The Name Above Every Name." Amazingly, he has more than six million followers.[10]

And in the United States, in South Florida, **José Luis de Jesús Miranda**, founder of the Growing in Grace movement, claimed to be Jesus Christ and the Antichrist at the same time.[11] He died in August 2013[12], and like all these other false christs, he has not come back to life. And like so many cult followers, his many followers had their false faith shattered.

In our increasingly biblically illiterate culture, more and more people are prone to follow false messiahs. As a matter of fact, LifeWay Research tells us that there may be up to five thousand cults in America today. Estimates show their followings are growing by 180,000 people a year.[13] Rational thinkers would think surely by now people would not be so gullible as to follow these megalomaniac cult leaders, but the number of cult leaders is only increasing.

Jesus very clearly said not to be deceived by the many imposters who claim to be the Christ. He also said not to be surprised, "For many will come in My name, saying, 'I am the Christ,' and will mislead many" (Matt. 24:5). God is the only one who truly knows the future.

Sign #2: Wars and Rumors of Wars

You will be hearing of wars and rumors of wars. See that you are not frightened, for those things must take place, but that is not yet the end. For nation will rise against nation, and kingdom against kingdom. (Matt. 24:6–7)

It is fascinating how wars and their casualties have increased over the last 150 years. Wars have occurred in every century, but the number in the last 150 years has skyrocketed. Look at these two graphs that give some historical insight.

Militarized Disputes between Pairs of Countries Since 1870

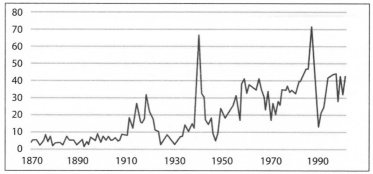

http://warwick.ac.uk/markharrison/data/frequency, Mark Harrision and Nikolaus Wolf

The frequency of wars increases and then declines, while the overall frequency continues to increase. Don't forget that. It is important.

War Deaths per Century, 1500–1995

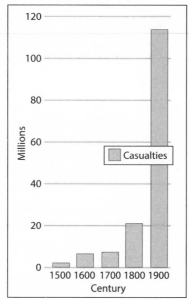

"Technology and War" by Alex Roland, http://www.unc.edu/depts/dipolomat

In a study by the University of North Carolina covering the casualties of war from the sixteenth to twentieth centuries, the increase is astounding.[14] Many scholars believe there were more casualties of war in the twentieth century than in all nineteen previous centuries since the time of Christ combined. Obviously, one reason is the increase in world population. Yet think what this says about what's ahead in the twenty-first century, when the world population is expected to grow from 7.3 billion in 2015 to 11.2 billion in 2100.[15] It will be a century in which more and more rogue nations will acquire nuclear bombs. When nations like Iran and others led by radical Islamists obtain nuclear weapons to join nations like North Korea, it makes me shudder to think of what may happen in the twenty-first century. After all, this is the century that began with the shock of 9/11.

Sign #3: Natural Disasters

And in various places there will be famines and earthquakes. (Matt. 24:7)

In other words, Jesus was describing the increase in natural disasters. The Emergency Disaster Database (EMDAT), maintained in Brussels, Belgium, indicates that "the total natural disasters reported each year has been steadily increasing in recent decades from 78 in 1970 to 348 in 2004."[16]

The number of natural disasters since 1900 has increased and then decreased, yet overall it has spiraled upward. When natural disasters hit—such as a hurricane like Katrina in 2004 or the great tsunami in Southeast Asia in 2004 or another in Japan in 2011 or the incredibly destructive and deadly tornadoes in the United States in 2011—we tend to think,

What's going on? I've never seen damage from nature's power like this.

Birth Pangs

Finally, Jesus said all these signs are like the beginning of birth pangs (Matt. 24:8). Of course, I've never had a baby. About 50 percent of the population can relate to that. My wife, however, experienced birth pangs with the delivery of our three sons. I have learned from her experience that at the onset of labor, the birth pangs are not that painful. They are also irregular in frequency. Then, as the birth of the baby gets closer, the birth pangs become more frequent and more intense. They intensify and subside, intensify and subside, with greater and greater intensity and frequency.

We were prepared for this as my wife and I waited for the birth of our first son. Like all good baby boomers, we attended a Lamaze class. We sat around the instructor along with eight or nine other couples holding pillows in our hands, learning how to breathe and push. I thought to myself, *All the way back to Neanderthal man people have been having babies, but we baby boomers think we need to have a class to learn how.*

Later on I realized these classes were as much for the men as for the mothers-to-be; we are supposed to be our wife's great encourager and source of support through the ordeal of labor. With our first child's birth, my role in labor and delivery was to rub my wife's back. After I had been doing that for a couple of hours, I complained to my wife, "This rubbing your back is wearing me out!" I have a great wife, a kind wife, a wife with a beautiful smile. But at that moment

23

in our marriage all I saw were ferocious daggers from her eyes, staring at me with rage. She replied, "It's making *you* tired?" It may have been one of the all-time stupid moments in the history of husbands. Thankfully, she was so focused on her pain that she couldn't kill me on the spot.

Jesus's insight on the signs of the times leading up to His second coming is amazing. He compared them to the birth pangs of a woman in labor, increasing in frequency and intensity as the birth approaches. And they are just like the increases in wars and natural disasters. Increase, then subside. Increase, then subside. But on an ever-increasing frequency and intensity until Jesus comes—like the birth pangs preceding the birth of a baby. There will be many difficult days. It will get worse and worse before relief comes. Then, like the joy of new life in the birth of a baby, Jesus will come to end the pain, fear, and evil in this world. He will bring judgment on evil and usher in a new age for all the earth when His kingdom finally comes.

Like a mother after the birth of her child, the pain will be quickly forgotten with the joy of Jesus's coming.

2

Is Anybody Listening?

The Silenced Suffering of Jesus's Followers

Jesus never sugar-coated His words:

> Then they will deliver you to tribulation, and will kill you, and you will be hated by all nations because of My name. (Matt. 24:9)

Whew! What an inspiring word in recruiting people to be His disciples.

"You'll face hard times when you follow me."
"You'll be killed for following me."
"You'll be hated by everyone if you follow me."

That doesn't sound like the health and wealth gospel or the shallow platitudes Christians often hear, such as "God wants you to be rich" or "your best is yet to be" or "become the better you," in the thousands of self-help books often disguised as biblical Christianity. Jesus wanted His disciples to know. Expect opposition! Expect persecution! Expect hardship! This will be the norm for Christians all through the ages.

The first-century disciples sure experienced tribulation. Historical tradition tells us that ten of the original eleven died a martyr's death for preaching the gospel (Judas, the twelfth, committed suicide after betraying Christ). The apostle John died in exile on the isle of Patmos.

First-century Christians were thrown to the lions by the Romans. Why? Because they were seen as traitors for not bowing to Caesar as God and instead believing in Jesus as Lord and God.

Yet, as tough as it was for the early Christians, the increase in persecution of Christians has intensified in the twentieth century. Catholic scholars believe more Christians were martyred in the twentieth century than in all previous centuries combined.[1] Marxism was the main perpetrator of this evil, especially in the old Soviet Union, China, North Korea, and Cambodia.

Yet, just as Marxism was the great evil in persecuting the church in the twentieth century, Islam is leading the slaughter and persecution of Christians and people of other religions in the twenty-first century. An estimated 4,344 Christians were martyred in 2014 as compared to 2,123 in 2013—a tremendous increase in just one year.[2]

I realize it may seem like nonsense to some to say that Marxism and Islam are very similar. In ideology, one is atheistic and one is based on a monotheistic belief in a god. Yet both are utopian ideologies that believe in the use of power to impose their beliefs on all the world.

In the summer of 2014, the civilized world was shocked as the Islamic State in Iraq and Syria (ISIS) or Islamic State in Iraq and the Levant (ISIL—another description of this radical Islamic group) stormed through Syria and Iraq like an unstoppable force. Along the way they sent out boastful videos in which soldiers beheaded British and American journalists. Amid this horror President Obama made a statement of outrage to the press saying, "One thing we can all agree on is that a group like ISIL has no place in the twenty-first century."[3] I sat stunned at the naiveté of his wishful thinking. The big story of the twenty-first century has been Islamic terrorism. It began in this century on 9/11 and hasn't let up—nor will it until all the world is brought into submission to Allah (*Islam* means "submission to Allah"). Then in February 2015, the western world was stunned to see an ISIS video that showed militants beheading twenty-one Egyptian Christian martyrs on a beach in West Libya. It's like the world has come full circle back to the first century. It is not what we want the world to be, but it is reality. This means persecution of the church will only get worse. Expect it. Jesus promised this in His prophecy on the signs of the times.

Doubly troubling is the lack of outrage in so-called "Christian America." Frank Wolf, a seventeen-term congressman from Virginia, who retired in 2014, probably has spoken out for religious liberty for all religions more over the last thirty years than any other American. He stood before the House of Representatives on July 31, 2014, to speak about the horrific bloodshed and suffering Christians and other religious groups were experiencing because of ISIS. He told of how the church in Mosul, Iraq's largest city, had been almost wiped out when these practitioners of the Qur'an and Hadith (their holy writings) demanded that Christians there convert to Islam, leave, or be killed. Wolf quoted columnist Kirsten Powers of

27

USA Today, who wrote, "Iraq's Christians are begging the world for help. Is anybody listening?" He concluded, "Mr. Speaker, this is the seventh consecutive legislative day that I have come to the House floor to ask that same question: Is anybody listening?"[4]

Another Sign (#4): Increasing Persecution

Congressman Wolf's question still lingers in my mind. For in light of Jesus's prophecy in Matthew 24:9, we need to be listening. The respect and freedom Christians in America have enjoyed for more than two hundred years is not the norm. As true Islam spreads, it won't be long in our increasingly clueless secular culture before we will be facing the type of persecution Christians have been facing in so many cultures over the last two thousand years.

Amazingly and ironically, on August 19, 2014, the *New York Times* ran an editorial by Ronald Lauder, president of the World Jewish Congress, that was titled, "Who Will Stand Up for the Christians?" He said, "Why is the world silent while Christians are being slaughtered in the Middle East and Africa? . . . The Middle East and parts of central Africa are losing entire Christian communities that have lived in peace for centuries. . . . The general indifference to ISIS, with its mass execution of Christians and its deadly preoccupation with Israel, isn't just wrong; it's obscene."[5] This is coming from not a Christian but a Jewish leader.

Yet the overwhelming majority of the "comfortable" American church seems uninformed and unconcerned about the persecution of Christians in our world. As ISIS engages in genocide with Christian communities in Syria and Iraq, many American Christians seem to be too weary of war in the Middle East to feel we can do anything about it. Yet we could—and we should. The famous words of Christian pastor Martin Niemöller in response to the Nazis of Hitler's Germany are relevant for today:

> First they came for the Socialists, and I did not speak out—
> Because I was not a Socialist.
> Then they came for the Trade Unionists, and I did not speak out—
> Because I was not a Trade Unionist.
> Then they came for the Jews, and I did not speak out—
> Because I was not a Jew.
> Then they came for me—and there was no one left to speak for me.[6]

These are sobering words for Western Christians as the genocide of Christians and other groups is taking place in the Middle East. It is simply delusional to feel this will never happen to us. Jesus warns His followers to expect tribulation.

If you claim to be a follower of Christ, will you be silent until it is too late?

Many Will Turn Away from God and the Church

> And you will be hated by all nations because of My name. At that time many will fall away and will betray one another and hate one another. (Matt. 24:9–10)

It has been said that persecution causes the church to grow. "The blood of the martyrs is the seed of the church."[7] Ironically, this is often true. When believers are genuine Christ-followers—loving those who persecute them and having no fear of death—many desire to have what they have, and the church, in many cases, does grow.

Yet Jesus said the opposite is also true. In many cases, the persecution is so difficult that many so-called professing Christians fall away and even turn on fellow Christians. Persecution has a way of cleansing the church and revealing who the true believers are. I believe that if American Christians experienced the same kind of persecution Christians do in Muslim-controlled nations, our membership rolls would be at best 10–20 percent of what they are today. American churches are overflowing with cultural Christians who are Christians in name only and are not true followers of Christ. When a price has to be paid to follow Jesus, many will fall away and even betray the Christians they know to escape persecution.

So how should we as Christians respond? First, don't take it personally. When people hate us for being a Christian, Jesus tells us they really hate Him (Matt. 24:9).

When a Christian is belittled, mocked, rejected, or excluded at school or the office or in the neighborhood, it's Jesus their persecutors hate. One of the original religious terrorists was a man named Saul, who was confronted by Jesus when he was on his way to Damascus, Syria, to persecute Christians. Jesus said to him that day, "Saul, Saul, why are you persecuting Me?" (Acts 9:4). It was a strange question to ask Saul, for he had not personally persecuted Jesus. Yet Jesus knew his hatred for Christians was really hatred for Him.

Now don't confuse this with a martyr's complex that many Christians take on because they act like self-righteous jerks.

If you are belittled, mocked, or rejected for being rude and self-righteous, please don't blame that on Jesus. That type of Christian needs to look in the mirror and confess to God that they have missed the true spirit and character of Jesus. They need to repent. True Christians will be persecuted for being Christlike. They will be opposed for sharing the gospel with nonbelievers.

Second, in our increasingly secular culture, the apostasy of the American church is happening right in front of our eyes. The church in America seems hell-bent on following the example of what has already happened to the church in Europe.

The increase of the "nones"—those with no belief in God and no affiliation with any church or synagogue—has skyrocketed in recent years. In 1990, 8 percent of Americans were in this category. By 2008, the number had almost doubled to 15 percent.[8] Astoundingly, just four years later in 2012, it had risen to almost 20 percent.[9] And by 2014, it had increased to almost 23 percent.[10] The falling away is occurring en masse in America, and the persecution has barely begun. What will it be like when true persecution becomes the norm? How can this be happening so dramatically and so quickly?

The Rise of False Prophets Who Will Mislead Many

Many false prophets will arise and will mislead many. (Matt. 24:11)

Just as there will be more and more false messiahs the closer we get to the end of the age, there also will be more and more false prophets. False prophets go all the way back to the first century. They have continued in every age.

The most influential false prophet in all of history was Mohammed, who founded Islam in the seventh century AD—about six hundred years after the coming of Christ. In 2015, there were more than 1.7 billion followers of this false prophet. Islam is second only to the number of those claiming to be Christians (more than two billion).[11] *USA Today* published an article on April 2, 2015, titled, "Islam Projected to be World's Largest Religion by 2070." Their report was based on the findings of the Pew Research Center that show Islam growing at a far greater rate than any other religion.

The most influential false prophet in American history was Joseph Smith, founder of the Mormon church (officially called The Church of Jesus Christ of Latter-day Saints). Yet Joseph Smith had much more in common with Mohammed than with Jesus. He, like Mohammed, had many wives. In November 2014, the Mormon church finally acknowledged he had up to forty wives, with the youngest bride being fourteen years old.[12] Mohammed's youngest bride was nine when the marriage was consummated.[13]

Early on, they both saw themselves not as founders of a new religion but as leaders purifying the corruption of Judaism and Christianity in Scripture. Both claimed to have received special revelations from God, and both authored authoritative books (the Qur'an and the Book of Mormon) that take numerous Old Testament and New Testament Scriptures out of context and often alter them. These books have greater authority to Muslims and Mormons than the Bible. For Christians, the Bible is the ultimate authority of what we believe and how we practice our faith.

Mohammed and Smith both justified the use of violence in defense of their religious beliefs. All these similarities between Mohammed and Joseph Smith are radically different from Jesus.

False prophets and messiahs will continue to multiply and attract followers outside and inside the church. The rise of apostasy in the European church in the twentieth century and now in twenty-first century America is largely because of false prophets within the church.

For example, the rise of liberal theology in the seminaries and pulpits of many mainline Protestant denominations has resulted in a groundswell of universalism in the pews, along with the endorsement of sexual immorality by so many "pro-sin" clergy.

Then there are the "self-help gospel" and "health and wealth gospel," often known as prosperity theology and the "feel good" gospel, which often fall under the guise of evangelical biblical Christianity but are clearly heresy nevertheless. No doubt many leading evangelical pastors will be joining the pro-sin clergy of mainline Protestants with the rationalization of reaching more people with the gospel. But it will be a false gospel from a false prophet that will lead many astray. Jesus warned against this.

Lawlessness Is Increased, While Most People's Love Grows Cold

> Because lawlessness is increased, most people's love will grow cold. But the one who endures to the end, he will be saved. (Matt. 24:12–13)

Whether or not you are a Christian, does any rational person believe America is more moral today than thirty, fifty, or seventy years ago? With more and more false prophets in our midst, it only makes sense that lawlessness will increase. Christ calls the church to be salt and light in a dark world. But when salt loses its savor, it is useless (Matt. 5:13). Such is the church that waters down Christian biblical teaching and begins to reflect the values of the world more than the teaching and values of Jesus.

Amid this scenario, people's love for the Lord begins to grow cold. Self-serving survival, materialism, and hedonism begin to take precedent. Does this describe you? Cultural Christianity, which can be defined as when a person claims to be a Christian but does not make following Jesus their priority, is epidemic in the American church today. It is a dangerous place to be spiritually. Only those who are genuine followers of Jesus will endure to the end. And only those truly saved through faith in Christ will last for eternity in following Jesus.

In the meantime, despite the increasing tribulation, false teaching, and apostasy, Jesus reminds His followers to stay focused on the mission. So what is this mission exactly?

3

The Urgency of the Mission

A Great and Pressing Commission

This gospel of the kingdom shall be preached in the whole world as a testimony to all the nations, and then the end will come. (Matt. 24:14)

No vision of Jesus is more important than this. Jesus commands us to preach "the gospel of the kingdom" to every nation. Then He gives one of His clearest statements on when "the end will come." What did Jesus mean by "the end will come"? The end of what? Roman rule over first-century Jews in Israel? Did the disciples think that? Or did He mean the end of the existence of the earth? The phrase "as a testimony" gives key insight. The church's "testimony" is the clear mission to preach the gospel to every people group on the planet. Then the end will come. He is speaking of the end of the world as we know it—when Jesus will come to establish His kingdom on earth as it is in heaven.

What Is the Gospel?

Gospel means "good news." But that concept is never adequately grasped until we realize it is good news that follows bad news. If your spouse had gone to work on an upper floor of the World Trade Center on 9/11, it would have been very bad news. Getting a call from your spouse telling you he or she was trapped would have been devastating news. Then seeing the towers of the World Trade Center crumble into rubble on television would have been horrific news. But later that day if your spouse had called and told you that he or she was one of the few rescued by the firefighters shortly before the towers collapsed, it would have been incredibly good news following all the bad news of that day.

That is what the gospel is. God's Word tells us that we are all sinners and our sins separate us from God (Rom. 3:23). This is bad news. The judgment of God on sin is death (Rom. 6:23). More bad news. But the good news that follows that bad news is God loves us so much that He gave His only Son to pay the penalty for our sins on a Roman cross (John 3:16). He died in our place to offer us the opportunity to be forgiven of all our sin and to make our relationship right with God. This good news keeps getting better. He also rose from the dead to conquer sin and death and offer us eternal life with Him. This eternal life is about an eternal relationship with God. Death conquers us all, but Christ has conquered death so that if we choose to believe in Christ and put our trust in Him through repentant faith, then we receive this great gift. Total forgiveness. A right relationship with God. Eternal life. That's a boatload of good news following the bad news. God never forces us to believe this good news or accept it. The decision is ours. No one can make the decision for you. Yet why in the world would anyone *not* want to receive this good news?

The Gospel of the Kingdom

Jesus didn't just speak of the gospel, but the gospel of the kingdom. When we individually trust Christ, we enter a large corporate body—the kingdom of God. Jesus's coming was the dawning of that kingdom.

So what is the kingdom of God? Theological tomes have been written to explain what it is, but here it is in a nutshell: the kingdom of God is wherever Jesus reigns. If Jesus reigns as Lord in your life, the kingdom of God is there. If He reigns in your family, the kingdom of God is there. If He reigns in a church or ministry, the kingdom of God is there. It is wherever Jesus reigns. Jesus did not come to establish denominations. He came for the dawning of the kingdom. Denominations have lasting value only if they are all about building up Christ's kingdom.

So when we pray, "Your kingdom come. Your will be done, on earth as it is in heaven" (Matt. 6:10), we are praying not only for Christ to come again and establish His Kingdom here on this earth but also for Him to reign in our lives, our families, and our churches. We are also praying a very evangelistic and missional prayer—that Christ will reign in our community, our nation, and in the lives of our friends and everyone from every people group on the face of the earth.

Preaching the Gospel to the Whole World

Many churches contend that "there are so many lost people in our community that we don't need to worry about the nations of the world." So they focus their ministries and financial resources on their own people or their own communities. This is pure disobedience to Jesus's Great Commission.

The local church is the local mission field where we are headquartered. Yet Christ not only commands us to love our neighbors, He commands us to preach the gospel to the whole world. This means every people group.

The word for "nation" in the Greek is *ethnos*. We get our word *ethnic* from it. This is key. Jesus knew that national boundaries and the names of nations would change all through the ages, but ethnic groups are more constant. This means Jesus was telling us to reach every people group on the face of the earth—people with common culture and a common language.

Missiologists have found that among the 7 billion people on planet Earth, there are more than 11,000 people groups. Of all the people groups, around 6,800 are considered unreached. What is an unreached people group? It's where less than 2 percent of the population is made up of Christ-followers.[1] By this definition, even Japan would be considered an unreached people group even though Japan has had a Christian witness for its nation for hundreds of years. Yet, far less than 2 percent of the Japanese population is Christian. That makes them a very large unreached people group.

Among the 6,800 unreached people groups, about 3,100 are considered unreached and unengaged. These groups that we'll call UUPGs (unreached and unengaged people groups) have no known Christian or ministry or church among the whole people group. Not only are they unreached, but also no one is engaging them with the gospel. Christ commissioned the church almost two thousand years ago, and still more than three thousand people groups have yet to have a single known Christian. This is unacceptable.

Yet here is what is amazing. In 2011, there were over 3,800 UUPGs. That means from 2011 to 2015, the number dropped by around 700. This is the fastest drop in the history of the church. God's Spirit is moving powerfully over the face of the earth, and no Christian wants to miss out on what He is doing.

Now I want to share a personal story. It was February 2011, while I was serving as president of the Southern Baptist Convention. Our local church was having its annual global missions conference. The Holy Spirit moved in me powerfully with this thought: *Our denomination has more than 45,000 churches. Surely 3,800 of those churches could each adopt one of these UUPGs to pray for the gospel to be preached among that people group. With those prayers would be a willingness for that church to send some of their own with the gospel.* The Lord clearly was leading me to challenge the churches of our convention at our annual meeting in Phoenix that June to rise up and adopt all 3,800 UUPGs. But there was a major issue. Our International Mission Board (IMB) would have to take on the huge logistical task of connecting churches that responded to that challenge to each specific people group. On top of that, the IMB had just named a new president, Tom Elliff, who hadn't even taken office. I knew I needed to give him a call and share what the Holy Spirit had put on my heart, even though we did not know each other well.

When I reached Tom by phone, I told him I knew this would be a mammoth undertaking for the IMB but was sure the Holy Spirit was calling me to challenge the churches of our convention to adopt all 3,800 unreached and unengaged people groups. *Silence*. My mind was racing. Was he thinking, *This is crazy. That would be an impossible task?* Finally, he responded, "Bryant, you are not going to believe this, but I've just spent the last two days meeting with all the vice presidents of the IMB and telling them the Lord is leading me to challenge the churches of our denomination to adopt all 3,800 unreached and unengaged people groups at this year's convention in Phoenix."

I could not speak. I began to silently weep. Discovering that the Holy Spirit is working in two different places with the same conviction unbeknownst to each other is an overwhelming experience. It left me speechless.

Tom issued that challenge, and more than 600 churches responded. Since that time, the number has grown to more than 1,800. And that is just one denomination.

It is so exciting to know that our denomination realizes that no one denomination or ministry can do this alone. More and more Great Commission Christian denominations and ministries around the world are feeling this calling. God is moving mightily in our age. If the number of UUPGs has dropped from more than 3,800 to about 3,100 in four years, then that means around 700 former UUPGs have Christians on the ground who are starting churches in homes and villages so those people groups can be reached with the gospel by their own people.

Given that around 700 UUPGs have been engaged with the gospel in the last four years, is it possible that the remaining 3,100 can be reached in our lifetime? What an exciting thought! What an opportunity for the church today!

When that is done, Jesus's words could not be clearer: "And then the end will come." This gives us urgency for completing our mission! If you are a Christ-follower, you and your church don't want to miss out on being a part of what God is doing in these end times. It calls for urgency from us. But most of all, it is urgent for those UUPGs. Christian theologian Carl F. H. Henry is often given credit for the insightful phrase, "The gospel is only good news if it gets there in time."[2]

And here's the big challenge. The remaining three thousand UUPGs have not been reached because they are difficult to reach. They are in remote, hard-to-get-to regions. Many are controlled by highly closed Muslim regimes or trapped by other false religions. The price is going to be great. Many who go will face opposition and great hardship. Many will be persecuted, and some will be killed. Yet, what a glorious day it will be when the task is finally done! For like a mother feels having finally given birth to a baby after the intense birth pangs of childbirth, Christians who have taken part in fulfilling Christ's mission will quickly forget the "birth pangs" and rejoice in the victory of Christ's kingdom coming at last to this world.

When we receive the gospel, we have eternal life. Death holds no fear. And the gospel is not to hoard, as most American Christians do. It is to share with every people group on the face of the earth. A movement to do so is happening in a supernatural way today. People are paying great costs and even more will be in the future. Yet even if the cost is death, Jesus has conquered death, and so will we.

One fine young minister on our church staff came to me to let me know he felt called to move his family to the Middle East to serve with ministries already on the ground trying to penetrate various Muslim people groups that are extremely difficult to engage. He said, "If those firefighters were willing to race into the towers of the World Trade Center on 9/11 to save as many as they could—knowing it could mean losing their lives—isn't it even more important for us to be willing to go to the hard places on the earth to share the gospel with people there so some can be saved, even if it costs us our lives?" He gets it. What a spirit! May it be the spirit of every Christian and every church that follows Jesus in this age.

Yet in the latter days of the church fulfilling its mission, a development will begin taking place that will make it increasingly difficult. A leader will enter the world's stage and captivate the masses and even enthrall many in the church. He will come as a political savior to bring order and hope in an increasingly chaotic world that seems to be rapidly falling out of control. He will appear to be for good, but he will be the well-disguised embodiment of evil.

His name is the Antichrist. His arrival on the world scene will be the most significant sign that all hell is about to break loose, shortly before Jesus returns.

4

The Dragon from the Sea

The Rise of the Antichrist

The Antichrist is the counterfeit Christ. He is the opposite of Christ. Just as Jesus is God in the flesh, the Antichrist will be the devil in the flesh—in the form of a man. Because he is the great counterfeiter, he will appear to be good. He will appear to be for world unity and for peace. Yet he will be for unity only around himself. Through great charisma, diplomatic skill, and consolidation of great worldly power and military might, he will seek to pull this off. He will be far greater than the Caesars or Hitlers of history, for he will be endowed with supernatural power (not from God but from the devil). He will even appear to be killed and come back to life again, thus imitating Christ's death and resurrection. All the while he will be seeking to do what the devil does—usurp God with his own arrogant greatness. He will be evil incarnate who will seek to rule the world through a one-world government of which he is the ruler.

All through history, Christians have made the mistake of trying to identify the Antichrist. This goes all the way back to the first century, when some Christians equated him with the Caesars of Rome. Taking on the title of "divine" and calling for submission to their rule in order to bring unity to the Roman Empire, it is easy to see why many Christians thought that various Caesars were the Antichrist. The Caesars were a type of Antichrist, but they were not the final one.

Fast-forward 1,500 years when the Roman Catholic Church had tremendous power over political and government systems in Europe. It had also become incredibly corrupt. It is easy to see why certain reformers, like Martin Luther, labeled the pope as the Antichrist. Luther came to think of the pope as the Antichrist because of the general tradition about where to find the Antichrist. The Antichrist was someone subverting the church from within. When he read the history of the papal office and saw it subverting the gospel as he understood it, Luther became convinced that the papal office was the office of the Antichrist.[1] Dennis Pettibone, in his article "Martin Luther's Views on the Antichrist," quotes Philip Cary, author of *Luther: Gospel, Law, and Reformation*, "The reformation wouldn't have happened without the conviction that the pope was the Antichrist."[2] When Luther got word that Pope Leo X was sending an edict to threaten him with excommunication, "All ambiguity about the Antichrist evaporated in his mind; to him the pope was the Beast, the man of evil foretold in the New Testament, and no compromise was possible."[3]

This mind-set toward the pope among many Protestants existed for almost five hundred years after Luther, even though many Protestants and evangelical Christians would feel embarrassed about that mind-set today. Obviously, no pope has proved to be the Antichrist.

With the rise of Adolf Hitler in World War II, some in the German army came to the conclusion that he was the Antichrist. No doubt he was certainly the greatest foreshadowing of the final Antichrist. He had hypnotic charisma and sought to unify Germany and Europe around himself. Combine that with his hatred of the Jews, and he seemed to be the perfect candidate. Yet as evil as he was, Hitler was not the final and ultimate Antichrist.

Christians in America have been known to demonize political leaders they don't like. I remember traveling to my wife's grandparents' home in Missouri during our first year of marriage. Having never been there, I wandered into the garage where I saw a picture of President Richard Nixon tacked to the wall. I walked over and saw that her grandfather, a loyal Democrat, had written the words *the Devil* all over his face. I thought two things. First, *I'm not going to bring up politics in this house*; second, *I doubt it*, as Nixon had recently resigned from office in disgrace. He may have been the devil incarnate to many Democrats and members of the press, but he was not the final and ultimate Antichrist.

The Bible introduces the Antichrist in Revelation 13:

> And the dragon stood on the sand of the seashore. Then I saw a beast coming up out of the sea, having ten horns and seven heads, and on his horns were ten diadems, and on his heads were blasphemous names. (Rev. 13:1)

Revelation contains a lot of symbolism, which is one of the major reasons people stay away from it. Some say, "It's just too difficult to understand" or "It has too many interpretations."

Certainly Revelation is not easy to follow, and there are many ways to interpret it. Yet there are some key points every serious scholar will agree on. It teaches that Jesus will come again. His second coming will be preceded by the rise of the Antichrist on the world's scene. This man's amazing supernatural power and leadership will allow him to swiftly unify the world around himself. He will eventually lead many nations of the world into the climactic battle of history in the Battle of Armageddon.

Revelation 13:1 introduces that Antichrist to the world scene with symbolic terminology. Yet as we'll see time and again, looking at Scripture in light of Scripture, the symbolism of prophecy becomes clear.

The Dragon

The dragon is clearly the devil. Scripture identifies him this way in Revelation 12:7–9:

> And there was war in heaven, Michael and his angels waging war with the dragon. The dragon and his angels waged war, and they were not strong enough, and there was no longer a place found for them in heaven. And the great dragon was thrown down, the serpent of old who is called the devil and Satan, who deceives the whole world; he was thrown down to the earth, and his angels were thrown down with him.

The devil was a very important angel in heaven who fell out of favor with God by falling in love with himself. He became filled with pride and wanted to usurp God. He led a rebellion in heaven among the angels. Evidently one-third of them followed him (Rev. 12:4). They were cast out of heaven.

We don't know exactly when, but we do know it occurred sometime before the devil tempted Eve to disobey God in the Garden of Eden (Gen. 3:1–7).

The devil is clearly identified as the dragon. This is example number one of studying Scripture in light of Scripture in order to understand the symbolism of Revelation.

The Sea

The dragon in Revelation 13:1 is described as standing on a seashore. The sea, biblically, stands for chaos. It sometimes stands for the world systems without God or man's restlessness without God. Sometimes in the morning, the ocean will look as smooth as glass. But it is an illusion. I realized that one day while trying to water ski on it. It was not fun. It almost beat me to death. The sea is always restless and unsettled. It can symbolize chaos and even the abyss.

The Beast

Revelation 13:1 also tells of a beast coming up out of the sea—out of the chaos and restlessness of the world. In Scripture, the beast is the Antichrist (Dan. 7:3; Rev. 15:2; 16:13; 17:8; 19:19–20).

When we think of a beast, we think of an unstoppable, powerful, ferocious animal. Revelation 13 paints a picture of this beast. He has ten horns and seven heads, and on his horns are ten diadems that have blasphemous names written on them. Obviously, the Antichrist will rule over ten great kingdoms. Blasphemy is mocking God or claiming to be God. It is espoused by those who feel greater than God and mock God's existence. This is certainly a character trait of the devil that got him kicked out of heaven.

What these kingdoms with seven heads are, we do not know. But in time all this will become clear:

> And the beast which I saw was like a leopard, and his feet were like those of a bear, and his mouth like the mouth of a lion. And the dragon gave him his power and his throne and great authority. (Rev. 13:2)

Revelation 13:2 tells us the beast (the Antichrist) is like a leopard and his feet are like those of a bear. His mouth is like that of a lion. What does this mean? Before we see the answer, Revelation 13:2 tells us that the devil will give the Antichrist his power, throne, and great authority. He will be the devil incarnate empowered by the prince of this world (the prince of this world is the devil, not Jesus).

Think of how often a new political leader comes onto the world scene with incredible charisma and power, managing to charm the nation into following him. This was certainly the case with President Obama when he packed the Broncos' Mile High Stadium in Denver to accept his party's nomination in 2008. It was an illustration of how often the world is longing for a dynamic leader to provide hope and comfort amid the chaos of our world. In the 2016 race for the White House, Bernie Sanders and Donald Trump amazingly had that kind of impact on their followers.

Now, obviously, President Obama is not the Antichrist. He's just a man who struggled to be a good president. But it is a reminder of that desperate longing in this restless, chaotic world for a leader to make it what we all deep down long for it to be.

Isn't it amazing how different Jesus is from the Antichrist? The Antichrist will be all about worldly power, but Jesus refused the devil's offer for the opportunity to rule the world with power and might (Matt. 4:8–10). All Jesus had to do was bow down to the devil. Think of what a temptation that was at the beginning of His ministry. He could have brought about world peace, ended world hunger, and eliminated poverty. On and on He could have rationalized this by thinking of all the good He could do. Yet He responded, "It is written, 'YOU SHALL WORSHIP THE LORD YOUR GOD AND SERVE HIM ONLY'" (Luke 4:8). Jesus is just the opposite of the Antichrist. Jesus chose the way of suffering, sacrifice, and the cross to fulfill His Father's will. While the Antichrist will want to unite the world through worldly power, Jesus rejected that in favor of fulfilling His Father's will with the cross. One day He will unite the world! What a contrast!

So if the Antichrist (the beast) is like a leopard, a lion, and a bear, what does this tell us? Once again, looking at Scripture in light of Scripture, the symbolism of Revelation is easily explained. Now we begin to see how the Old Testament constantly gives insight to New Testament prophecy. The prophet Daniel explains it. He doesn't tell us who the Antichrist is, but he does provide insight into what the Antichrist will be like and where he will appear on the world scene.

5

Kingdoms Falling Down

A Foreshadowing of the Antichrist

Daniel is the last of the four Major Prophets, including Isaiah, Jeremiah, and Ezekiel. These prophets are called "major" because they were long-winded (or wrote longer books). Minor Prophets wrote shorter books. Yet they all are important. Few prophets provide more insight about end times prophecy than Daniel.

Daniel was a brilliant Jewish man who served as a powerful minister in the king's court of ancient Babylon. That king was Nebuchadnezzar, the most powerful man in the world, for Babylon was the dominant world power of its day—much like the United States is today. Ancient Babylon was located in what is now modern-day Iraq. So it is little wonder that Nebuchadnezzar was Saddam Hussein's hero. Saddam wanted to lead Iraq back to greatness similar to what Babylon experienced under Nebuchadnezzar.

In 605 BC, Nebuchadnezzar put Jerusalem under siege. When he did that, he took some of the most prominent and best educated Jews back to Babylon. This was the beginning of the Babylonian captivity of the Jews that reached its peak in 587 BC, when Nebuchadnezzar completely destroyed Jerusalem and the magnificent temple Solomon had built on what is today called the Temple Mount.

Daniel was among the Jews that Nebuchadnezzar took into captivity in 605 BC. His story is inspiring because even as a young man being trained in the court of Nebuchadnezzar, he never compromised his faith, and God blessed him for it (Dan. 1–6).

When Daniel was able to interpret Nebuchadnezzar's dreams, he rose to great power in the king's court. This didn't sit well with the Babylonians. It would have been like Saddam Hussein capturing an Israeli-Jewish soldier in the 1990s who proved to be so bright and helpful that he became a key member of his cabinet. I doubt the Iraqis in Saddam's cabinet would have been very happy about that, especially since so many Muslims dislike the Jews. This explains how amazing Daniel's power was in Babylon.

Yet in Daniel 7, it is not a Babylonian king who has a vision, it is Daniel. Because it occurred at night, it was probably a dream. God had gifted Daniel with interpreting dreams, so he shared this vision (dream) and sought to interpret it. Revelation 13 introduced us to the Antichrist, called the "beast." Now Daniel writes of four great beasts coming up out of the sea. So are there four beasts or one? What we'll see is a foreshadowing of the final and ultimate beast—the Antichrist:

Daniel said, "I was looking in my vision by night, and behold, the four winds of heaven were stirring up the great sea. And four great beasts were coming up from the sea, different from one another." (Dan. 7:2–3)

He tells of the wind stirring the sea. So often in Scripture, the wind is symbolic of the Holy Spirit (John 3:5–8). The sea, remember, represents chaos and worldly systems without God. This picture in verse 2 shows that God is in charge of history. Even out of the chaos of worldly systems, God's plan for history will be fulfilled.

Then Daniel describes four great beasts coming out of the sea. The first three are a foreshadowing of the last great beast—the Antichrist. This means they are world leaders who give us a picture of what the final Antichrist will be like. All four kingdoms are a foreshadowing of what the final Antichrist kingdom longs to be—a one-world government. This will be a government that he will seek to be composed of all the nations of the world and ruled by the Antichrist. All nations, then, will probably include the United States, if we are still around.

The First Beast: Nebuchadnezzar

The first beast is like a lion. This sounds like Revelation 13:2. Only this lion has "the wings of an eagle." Daniel goes on, "I kept looking until its wings were plucked, and it was lifted up from the ground and made to stand on two feet like a man; a human mind also was given to it" (Dan. 7:4). This is clearly symbolic of Babylon and Nebuchadnezzar.

Remember, Old Testament prophets were not just predictors of the future. They most of all spoke God's Word to the present situation of their day. Yet because they spoke the eternal word of God, their prophecy would often have future ramifications and insight. As we'll see, this was certainly the case with Daniel.

How do we know the lion with wings of an eagle represents Babylon and the man represents Nebuchadnezzar? Jeremiah, another Old Testament Jewish prophet, refers to the Babylonian kingdom as the lion (Jer. 4:7; 50:17, 44). But even more important, historians tell us that the symbol of the Babylonian kingdom was a lion with eagle's wings.[1] So when Daniel wrote this prophecy, it would have been common knowledge that the lion with eagle's wings symbolized Babylon and its ferocious greatness and power.

It is also interesting that Daniel earlier predicted that when Nebuchadnezzar was at the peak of his power, he would go mad (Dan. 4:1–27). Amazingly, that is exactly what happened:

Twelve months later he was walking on the roof of the royal palace of Babylon. The king reflected and said, "Is this not Babylon the great, which I myself have built as a royal residence by the might of my power and for the glory of my majesty?" While the word was in the king's mouth, a voice came from heaven, saying, "King Nebuchadnezzar, to you it is declared: sovereignty has been removed from you, and you will be driven away from mankind, and your dwelling place will be with the beasts of the field. You will be given grass to eat like cattle, and seven periods of time will pass over you until you recognize that the Most High is ruler over the realm of mankind and bestows it on whomever He wishes." Immediately the word concerning Nebuchadnezzar was fulfilled; and he was driven away from mankind and began eating grass like cattle, and his body was drenched with the dew of heaven until his hair had grown like eagles' feathers and his nails like birds' claws. (Dan. 4:29–33)

This is clearly what Daniel was referring to in Daniel 7:4 when he writes that he saw that the lion's wings were plucked.

The Second Beast: The Medo-Persian Empire

And behold, another beast, a second one, resembling a bear. And it was raised up on one side, and three ribs were in its mouth between its teeth; and thus they said to it, "Arise, devour much meat!" (Dan. 7:5)

This second beast symbolizes the Medo-Persian Empire. How do we know this?

1. Daniel 7:17 explains the four beasts in Daniel's vision. They represent the four great world powers in history from Daniel's day forward:

   These great beasts, which are four in number, are four kings who will arise from the earth. (Dan. 7:17)

2. History tells us that the Babylonian Empire was conquered in 539 BC by Cyrus the Great, the leader of the Medo-Persian Empire that became known as the Persian Empire. Today the Persian people are found in Iran. The modern world clearly remembers the brutal and gruesome war between Iraq and Iran that lasted for most of the 1980s. It began in September 1980 and wasn't over until August 1988.[2] But what most Americans do not realize is that the hostility between these two nations goes all the way back to when they battled it out in Daniel's day (sixth century BC) to be the dominant power in all the world. The modern conflict in the 1980s was greatly exacerbated because Hussein, a Sunni Muslim of Iraq,

despised the Ayatollah Khomeini's Shiite Muslims of Iran and Iraq.

The ancient Persian Empire lasted two hundred years. It was one of the greatest empires in all of history. At one point, it was almost as expansive as the Roman Empire. Along with its size, it was a very sophisticated culture that would influence the Greeks and Romans that followed.

In Daniel 7:5, the second beast in Daniel is described as a bear with three bloody ribs in its mouth. It is interesting that the Persian Empire had three great victories that led them to become the dominant empire in all the earth. The first was their victory over the Lydians (modern-day Turkey) in 546 BC. The second was over the Babylonians in 539 BC. The third great victory was over Egypt when Egypt was at the tail end of its great empire in 525 BC.[3]

The Third Beast: Alexander the Great and Greece

The third great beast is described as a leopard in Daniel 7:6:

> After this I kept looking, and behold, another one, like a leopard, which had on its back four wings of a bird; the beast also had four heads, and dominion was given to it.

This beast clearly represents Alexander the Great and the Greeks. Alexander the Great conquered the Persians in 331 BC to make Greece the dominant empire on the planet. He was known to gobble up real estate so quickly that he is compared to a leopard, which is a lightning-fast beast of prey. He was such a mighty conqueror that he had conquered the known world by the time he was almost thirty-three years old.

Tradition says that he then wept because there were no more worlds to conquer.[4] He conquered with such speed that the only comparison from the twentieth century is Hitler, who stormed quickly through Europe. Later, on a micro scale, the world saw ISIS (ISIL) storming through parts of Syria and Iraq in 2014 and 2015 at the speed of a leopard. This gave the world another taste of gobbling up great swaths of real estate at lightning speed.

When Alexander died at age thirty-three, his empire stretched over 10,000 miles—all the way into India. It was far too vast for one man to rule, which is why Daniel 7:6 is so interesting when it says, "the beast also had four heads, and dominion was given to it." Long after Daniel the prophet had died, this prophecy would be fulfilled when Alexander the Great died and his empire was divided into four parts in 323 BC. These four parts would be ruled by four men. This Greek kingdom would be dominant in the world until Rome conquered it in 146 BC.

What is so interesting about these three great kingdoms made famous by the rule of three great men was that the rulers sought to unify the world around themselves through political power and might. Nebuchadnezzar and Alexander the Great especially saw themselves as "divine-like," having egos so great they felt they were greater than God. These character traits are a foreshadowing of the final and ultimate Antichrist.

Then comes the fourth beast described in Daniel 7:7. It is a beast so terrifying and awesome that no animal symbolism is adequate:

> After this I kept looking in the night visions, and behold, a
> fourth beast, dreadful and terrifying and extremely strong;

and it had large iron teeth. It devoured and crushed and trampled down the remainder with its feet; and it was different from all the beasts that were before it, and it had ten horns.

Hollywood today has a genre of apocalyptic movies that often feature courageous good guys battling an evil force that is beastlike, terrifying, and unstoppable.

This last beast described in Daniel clearly represents the ancient Roman Empire that conquered the Greeks in 146 BC. It would become the greatest and most powerful empire in world history. It would also last the longest. According to historians, its western portion lasted six hundred years until it was conquered by the Goths when it was crumbling from within in the fifth century AD. Its eastern portion lasted 1600 years until it was conquered by the Muslim Ottoman Turks in ancient Constantinople (modern-day Istanbul) in May 1453.

Yet what historians say was the end of the western and eastern portions of the Roman Empire is refuted by Daniel the prophet. Was he wrong? God's Word never is. For the world has not seen the end of the Roman Empire, and from its modern-day revival will come the ultimate and final Antichrist.

6

A Beast Unlike Any Before

The Roman Empire and Today

By now, you may be wondering, *How can we know for sure that the beasts of the lion, the bear, and the leopard represent Babylon, Persia, and Greece?* God's Word through Daniel clearly provides insight:

> As for me, Daniel, my spirit was distressed within me, and the visions in my mind kept alarming me. I approached one of those who were standing by and began asking him the exact meaning of all this. So he told me and made known to me the interpretation of these things: "These great beasts, which are four in number, are four kings who will arise from the earth." (Dan. 7:15–17)

Knowing that Daniel lived and served in two great king-doms—Babylon and Persia—historians and Bible scholars are unanimous regarding whom he is talking about.

The fourth beast of Daniel's vision is the most important. Why? Because, as biblical scholars point out, it clearly represents the Roman Empire, yet no ultimate and final Antichrist arose from it. Yes, the Caesars with their claims of divinity (often with the help of the Roman Senate) certainly displayed the Antichrist-type character traits. But as evil as some of them were, none were the ultimate and final Antichrist. Yet Daniel 7:7–8 and 15–27 are quite clear that this person will come out of this fourth kingdom, the Roman Empire. How can this be?

> After this I kept looking in the night visions, and behold, a fourth beast, dreadful and terrifying and extremely strong; and it had large iron teeth. It devoured and crushed and trampled down the remainder with its feet; and it was different from all the beasts that were before it, and it had ten horns. While I was contemplating the horns, behold, another horn, a little one, came up among them, and three of the first horns were pulled out by the roots before it; and behold, this horn possessed eyes like the eyes of a man and a mouth uttering great boasts. (Dan. 7:7–8)

The fourth beast will be more "dreadful and terrifying" than the previous three. Daniel adds that it will be "extremely strong." It has "iron teeth" and tramples down and crushes and devours all in its path.

Then Daniel says something similar to the revelation of the final and ultimate Antichrist in Revelation 13:1: He will have "ten horns."

Daniel also writes of another horn, a little one that rises among the ten and evidently conquers or eliminates three of the existing horns. This horn has the "eyes of a man" and "a mouth uttering great boasts." Obviously, this horn represents the Antichrist who will start small among some confederation of ten kings but will rise quickly to power, eliminating three of the existing kings. So how do we reconcile that this fourth kingdom, the Roman Empire, ended in AD 476 in the west and AD 1453 in the east, and no final Antichrist emerged? Daniel explains:

> I kept looking until thrones were set up, and the Ancient of Days took His seat; his vesture was like white snow and the hair of His head like pure wool. His throne was ablaze with flames, its wheels were a burning fire. A river of fire was flowing and coming out from before Him; thousands upon thousands were attending Him, and myriads upon myriads were standing before Him; the court sat, and the books were opened.
>
> Then I kept looking because of the sound of the boastful words which the horn was speaking; I kept looking until the beast was slain, and its body was destroyed and given to the burning fire. As for the rest of the beasts, their dominion was taken away, but an extension of life was granted to them for an appointed period of time.
>
> I kept looking in the night visions, and behold, with the clouds of heaven one like a Son of Man was coming, and He came up to the Ancient of Days and was presented before Him. And to Him was given dominion, glory and a kingdom, that all the peoples, nations and men of every language might serve Him. His dominion is an everlasting dominion which will not pass away; and His kingdom is one which will not be destroyed. (Dan. 7:9–14)

In this passage, Jesus is described as "the Ancient of Days," who will come and slay the Antichrist. When Jesus comes,

He will establish His eternal kingdom composed of people from every people group on the face of the earth. He is the only man who is capable and called by God to rule all the nations of the world one day (thus, His imposter is called the Antichrist). Christ's kingdom is the only kingdom that will never be destroyed. All other earthly kingdoms—no matter how great—are only temporal.

Daniel writes that this vision distressed and alarmed him:

> As for me, Daniel, my spirit was distressed within me, and the visions in my mind kept alarming me. (Dan. 7:15)

So he asked for the exact meaning and interpretation of this terrifying vision:

> I approached one of those who were standing by and began asking him the exact meaning of all this. So he told me and made known to me the interpretation of these things. (Dan. 7:16)

The Meaning of the Vision (Dan. 7:17–27)

Daniel 7:17 offers a clear explanation of the fourth beast:

> These great beasts, which are four in number, are four kings who will arise from the earth.

Daniel writes of four great dominant kingdoms of this world, beginning with Nebuchadnezzar and the Babylonian Empire. This kingdom is followed by the Persian Empire. Amazingly, Daniel served kings in both of these great empires. The Persians' kingdom was followed by Alexander the Great and the Greeks. Then the Roman Empire with its many Caesars followed Greece. With Daniel only experiencing the Babylonian and Persian Empires, it reminds us of the miracle of biblical prophecy. God revealed the prophecy to the prophet even if the prophet couldn't fully understand it like we do today on the other side of history. It is so supernatural that when I was a student in the misery of a liberal seminary, most of the Old Testament professors were convinced that Daniel wasn't really written by Daniel who lived in the sixth century BC. They said his book is so accurate in describing these four great kingdoms that it had to have been written in the first century BC, after all these kingdoms had emerged on the world scene. They hypothesized that the writer just used Daniel's name. Obviously, they did not believe in the supernatural dimension of biblical prophecy, which makes for a little bitty god. This is very unlike the God of Scripture who sees all, knows all, and is over all the events of history—past, present, and future. Those professors spent their lives teaching the word of God while only believing the Word of God if there was a rational explanation. They seemed to have forgotten the part in the Word of God that says, "For nothing will be impossible with God" (Luke 1:37).

Daniel pursued more understanding about his vision of the fourth beast in verses 19–20, which are basically a repeat of verses 7–8:

> Then I desired to know the exact meaning of the fourth beast, which was different from all the others, exceedingly dreadful, with its teeth of iron and its claws of bronze, and which devoured, crushed and trampled down the remainder with its feet, and the meaning of the ten horns that were on its head and the other horn which came up, and before which three of them fell, namely, that horn which had eyes

and a mouth uttering great boasts and which was larger in appearance than its associates.

This fourth beast in verse 21 will wage war with the saints and overpower them:

I kept looking, and that horn was waging war with the saints and overpowering them.

Obviously, this happened with the Caesars of Rome and the early church. Yet even the Caesars never completely overpowered the church. As a matter of fact, we could make a case that the church overpowered Rome. In AD 324, when Constantine was the emperor of Rome, he began to advance the idea of the Roman Empire embracing Christianity. He even oversaw the building of a new basilica on Vatican Hill, where Peter was believed to have been martyred. Later in AD 380, Emperor Theodosius, an ardent Christian, made Christianity the official religion of the empire.[1]

Daniel 7:23–25 gives more insight into the fourth beast:

Thus he said: "The fourth beast will be a fourth kingdom on the earth, which will be different from all the other kingdoms and will devour the whole earth and tread it down and crush it. As for the ten horns, out of this kingdom ten kings will arise; and another will arise after them, and he will be different from the previous ones and will subdue three kings. He will speak out against the Most High and wear down the saints of the Highest One, and he will intend to make alterations in times and in law; and they will be given into his hand for a time, times, and half a time."

Rome was the world's greatest empire, but it was never as great as what Daniel describes in verse 23. It covered a lot of real estate in North Africa, most of Europe, and a small slice of Ethiopia, but it never included the Americas or Central and Southern Africa or most of Asia and Australia. It never ruled the world, but verse 23 says the fourth beast will.

The ten horns described in Revelation 13:1 and Daniel 7:7–8, 19–20, and the little horn that rises up and subdues three of the kingdoms, is described in Daniel 7:25 in four ways.

1. He will speak out against the Most High (obviously, God in Jesus Christ).
2. He will also wear down Christ-followers (implying a persecution of the church like the world has never known).
3. He will intend to alter the times and laws.
4. He will be given this great authority for "time, times, and half a time." Most biblical scholars believe this describes three and a half years. (This will become clear as we study Scripture in light of Scripture in Daniel 12:11 and Revelation 13:5.)

He is the Antichrist.

Daniel 7:26–27

We once again see a description of Jesus's second coming that is also described in detail in Revelation 19:11–21:

> But the court will sit for judgment, and his dominion will be taken away, annihilated and destroyed forever. Then the sovereignty, the dominion and the greatness of all the kingdoms under the whole heaven will be given to the people of the saints of the Highest One; His kingdom will be an

everlasting kingdom, and all the dominions will serve and obey Him. (Dan. 7:26–27)

Yet the Roman Empire died and no Antichrist emerged. Jesus never returned during those years. Is Scripture wrong? Was the prophet Daniel mistaken? No! At some point in history there will be a revival of the ancient Roman Empire from which the Antichrist will emerge.

All through European history, there has been this longing for the restoration of the greatness of the Roman Empire.

Charles the Great became king of France in AD 768. He is known to the world as Charlemagne. He was not only an extremely gifted leader but also a great warrior. His grandfather, Charles Martel, a devoted Christian, had defeated the Spanish Moors (Muslims who had conquered Spain). This halted the spread of Islam into Western Europe.[2] Otherwise, most everyone in Europe, and later North and South America, would have grown up attending a mosque rather than a church. On Christmas Day in AD 800 in the basilica of Rome, Pope Leo III crowned Charlemagne "Emperor of the Romans."[3] To this day he is called the Father of Modern Europe.[4]

In 1693, after looking at the devastation of war in Europe, William Penn, prime minister of England, called for a European Parliament that would prevent further wars.

In 1804, Napoleon had himself crowned as the Emperor of France, and later began calling for a United States of Europe. He said, "I wished to found a European system, a European code of laws, a European judiciary: there would be one people in Europe."[5]

In 1871, Otto von Bismarck of Germany conquered France, which led to the establishment of the Second Reich.[6] It had been almost a thousand years since Charlemagne established the Holy Roman Empire. So his empire was to begin the second thousand years. It didn't work out too well for him.

Adolf Hitler acted on the dream of a unified Europe by not only seizing control of Germany but also seeking to conquer all of Europe and unify it around himself. He had powerful charisma. I do not understand a word of German, but I find myself captivated while watching films of him making a speech. What passion! Out of respect to his predecessor, Otto Von Bismarck, who called for a Second Reich, Hitler called for a Third Reich, meaning a thousand-year reign over Europe. Remember, the Antichrist is the counterfeit Christ. (Scripture tells us in Revelation 20 no less than six times that when Jesus comes again, He will reign over all the earth for one thousand years.) With Hitler being a type of Antichrist, it only makes sense that his vision called for a thousand-year reign. Even though Adolf Hitler is the clearest foreshadowing of what the final Antichrist will be like, he was not the final and ultimate one.

In November 1945, Sir Winston Churchill stated in a speech to both houses of the Belgian parliament, "I see no reason why, under the guardianship of a world organization, there should not arise the United States of Europe, which will unify this continent in a manner never known since the fall of the Roman Empire."[7]

The European Economic Community (EEC), or Common Market, was founded on March 25, 1957, with a treaty in Rome that included France, West Germany, Italy, the Netherlands, Belgium, and Luxembourg.[8] The European Common Market became the European Community when the Maastricht Treaty, signed in Maastricht, Netherlands, went into force in 1993.[9] That treaty called for a common currency for all of Europe. In 1999, the euro was introduced as the common monetary unit of Europe.[10] It quickly caught on and remains the common currency today.

On October 29, 2004, the prime ministers and presidents of twenty-five European nations gathered together in Rome for the signing of the Constitution of the European Union. Even though that constitution made no mention of God or its Christian heritage, to the protest of the pope, Rome was selected for the signing, for it symbolized the center of European heritage and was seen as the religious capital of Europe. Yet each nation had to ratify it, and because the French and Dutch voters rejected it, another "Treaty of Lisbon" was signed in December 2007, eventually ratified by all, and entered into force in December 2009.[11]

While the longing for a united Europe is still in full force today, Great Britain voted to exit the European Union in a national referendum on June 23, 2016. This vote surprised the leaders of Britain (who were heavily opposed to their exit).[12] Yet because Britain's exit was over immigration and European bureaucracy, without a clear, strong leader, it only reinforces the longing for a strong leader. Temporary setbacks from a one-world government and a one-world leader are like "birth pangs."

So what do we make of all these current and historical events in light of biblical teaching?

1. Daniel the prophet tells of three great beasts that will be the foreshadowing of the fourth beast. This beast will be the ultimate and final Antichrist.

2. The Antichrist will arise out of the ancient Roman Empire that officially ended in AD 476 in the west and AD

1453 in Constantinople in the east. Yet no final Antichrist emerged.

3. Obviously, Scripture teaches some sort of revival of that fourth kingdom in Daniel that we know to be the Roman Empire.

4. That fourth kingdom's revival only makes sense as the European Union today. It not only represents much of what the Roman Empire was but also sees Rome as central to its heritage. With Europe's secular mind-set and a growing Muslim population whose religion is truly "Antichrist," it will be interesting to see this unfold.

5. Yes, we don't understand clearly at this date what the ten kingdoms are that are mentioned in Daniel 7 and Revelation 13:1. And yes, we do not know who the Antichrist is. But this we do know: with every generation there is greater and greater illumination of the unchanging biblical truth. When we study current world events, more and more of the mysteries of biblical prophecy are revealed to believers. We know more about Isaiah's and Daniel's prophecies than Isaiah and Daniel did. And since 1948, when Israel became a nation again after not existing for about 1,800 years, multiple biblical prophecies can now be realized that were simply inconceivable before. Biblical illumination continues to unfold in every generation as eyes are watching current world events through the biblical lens of unchanging truth.

6. In the meantime, as the identity of the final Antichrist is still only wonder and speculation, Christians want to take the words of Scripture seriously. The New Testament is clear regarding the spirit of the Antichrist that is in the world today:

> Children, it is the last hour; and just as you heard that
> antichrist is coming, even now many antichrists have
> appeared; from this we know that it is the last hour.
> Who is the liar but the one who denies that Jesus is the
> Christ? This is the antichrist, the one who denies the
> Father and the Son. (1 John 2:18, 22)

The spirit of the Antichrist is denying Jesus the Messiah.
It is denying that Jesus and God the Father are one. This
means atheists, agnostics, secularists, and other religions of
the world represent the spirit of the Antichrist when they do
so. That separates the sheep and the goats. The saved and the
lost. It clearly puts all humankind into one of two groups:
those who believe Jesus is the Messiah and God's Son and
those who do not.

First John 4:2–3 relates the same theme:

> By this you know the Spirit of God: every spirit that confesses
> that Jesus Christ has come in the flesh is from God; and every
> spirit that does not confess Jesus is not from God; this is
> the spirit of the antichrist, of which you have heard that it
> is coming, and now it is already in the world.

Those who say Jesus is not God's Son have the spirit of
the Antichrist. When we talk to Muslim friends and acquaintances, remember Islam teaches that Jesus is a great prophet
but not as great as Mohammed and is clearly not God's Son.
This is the spirit of the Antichrist. Every other religion denies
that Jesus is the Messiah and God's Son.

Friends and acquaintances of other religions may mean
well, but they are captives of the spirit of this world. Unlike
the spirit of this world, the Holy Spirit reveals to us that
Jesus is God.

So how do we respond to friends and acquaintances? We are called to love them while hating the false doctrine that blinds them to the truth. Scripture tells us not to be intimidated. "Greater is He who is in you than he who is in the world" (1 John 4:4). Yes, the majority of the world is captive of the evil one. They live in spiritual darkness. Yet Jesus Christ and the good news of the gospel can overcome that darkness and free them from enslavement to a false philosophy or religion.

When the final Antichrist comes, Christians will be able to recognize who he is by what God's Word tells us about him. Knowing and believing God's Word keeps us from being caught by surprise. It keeps us from being afraid. God's Word repeatedly tells us that Jesus will come and have the final say, and the Antichrist will be doomed. Beware of cultural Christians who believe people are Christian from birth (impossible), family heritage (impossible), or denominational traditions (impossible). If you do not know Jesus as Savior and Lord and believe His Word is the source for direction and understanding in life, you too can be deceived by the spirit of the Antichrist in any age. Will you?

7

Can One Man Rule the World?

How the Stage Is Set for the Ultimate Takeover

Abu Bakr Al-Baghdadi is a name still not that familiar to many Americans. Yet the movement he leads is well known. He is the self-proclaimed leader of ISIS, the Islamic State of Iraq and Syria. By the time you read this, he may be dead. Yet in 2014, ISIS stormed into the world's scene like a meteor lighting up the sky. President Obama chose to label it ISIL, the Islamic State of Iraq and the Levant, which really is a more appropriate choice. What is the Levant? It is the broad swath of real estate called the Middle East that extends from Egypt to Turkey. Sources differ on which countries comprise the Levant but often include some or all of these: Syria; Iraq; Jordan; Lebanon; Palestine; Israel; Cyprus; and portions of Turkey and Egypt.

This is important in order to understand the establishment of the caliphate, the Islamic state. It is to be led by the caliph. And who is he? He is the successor to Mohammed. The decision regarding who the successor to Mohammed would be after his death led to a violent disagreement that continues to this day. When Mohammed died in AD 632, he had not been clear about his successor.

Abu Bakr (does that name sound familiar?), Mohammed's father-in-law, first claimed the title of caliph in AD 632. He sought to put down the rebellions to his leadership and began a war of conquest for Islam. Why? Because Islam means submission. It is all about bringing the Middle East (and eventually the whole world) under submission to Allah. Abu Bakr ruled for only two years before he died. His successor, Umar, was a brilliant military and political strategist who conquered land all over the Middle East that even included Egypt in AD 642 and Persia (now Iran) in AD 643.[1] With his death, a huge disagreement arose between the leaders of Islam. Some felt the caliph should be a relative of Mohammed. That group rallied around Ali, a son-in-law of Mohammed. Others felt he should be chosen from among key leaders of Islam. From the former group came the Shiites. From the latter group came the Sunnis. These are the two major groups of Islam that are still battling violently for the leadership of "true" Islam.

The majority of Muslims are Sunnis, probably 85–90 percent. The Middle Eastern countries with the greatest percentage of Sunnis are Egypt, Jordan and Saudi Arabia, with Sunnis making up 90 percent or more of their population.[2] Shiites dominate in Iran and much of Iraq. Thus, we see why Iran and Saudi Arabia are continually at odds. The United

States' role with these two nations continues to exacerbate that rivalry.

All this background is important, because the leader of ISIL, Abu Bakr Al-Baghdadi—with the same first name as the first caliph after Mohammed and the godfather of the Sunnis—is a Sunni Muslim. He sees himself as bringing the Muslim world together under his rule. Then once that is done, he will bring together the world as a whole. Remember, Islam, like Marxism, is a utopian ideology that seeks to impose its principles on the whole world through power and force. One is in the name of God. One is atheistic. But their motive and methodology are demonically similar.

This raises the following question: Can one man rule the world? Is it even a remote possibility? I doubt it will be Abu Bakr Al-Baghdadi, for his leadership is intensely opposed by many not only in the Muslim world but also in the Western world. But if not him, could someone else make it happen someday? The Bible tells us clearly and emphatically, yes. His name is the Antichrist.

It is interesting that the character traits of the Antichrist in Scripture are quite similar to what Islam calls the Mahdi, the Twelfth Imam. Michael Youssef writes, "Muslims see the Mahdi as a savior who will lead a global revolution and establish a worldwide Islamic empire. The Mahdi will rule the earth as the final Caliph of Islam . . . The parallels between the biblical Antichrist and the Madhi of Islam are chilling. Both are associated with the end times and the Judgment. Both possess political, military, and religious power."[3] This is interesting in light of current events, but one thing is for sure—the Bible is clear. The Antichrist will precede the second coming of Jesus.

We saw how Revelation 13:1–2 introduces the Antichrist to the world scene as a pivotal character who will precede the second coming of Jesus. Yet with so many opposing national interests, how could it ever happen?

As the world becomes more and more chaotic, there will be an increasing longing to turn to one man to bring order and unity out of the chaos. Adolf Hitler was this man to Germany in the Great Depression of the 1930s. Abu Bakr Al-Baghdadi has the same type of ambition that Hitler had. Only time will tell if he is capable of assimilating the same type of power. But one day, when the situation is right, an extraordinarily gifted man with supernatural abilities will emerge onto the world scene to seize political power and might to unify the world around himself. He will be far greater than Nebuchadnezzar, Alexander the Great, the Caesars of Rome, Napoleon, or Hitler.

God's Word describes what the world will be like in those days in 2 Timothy 3:1–5. The days will be very difficult:

> But realize this, that in the last days difficult times will come. For men will be lovers of self, lovers of money, boastful, arrogant, revilers, disobedient to parents, ungrateful, un-holy, unloving, irreconcilable, malicious gossips, without self-control, brutal, haters of good, treacherous, reckless, conceited, lovers of pleasure rather than lovers of God, hold-ing to a form of godliness, although they have denied its power; Avoid such men as these.

People Will Be Lovers of Self

Humans have always been lovers of self because of their sin nature. Yet in the "last days," the self-love will be far more unrestrained. The mind-set will more and more be "all about me." This mind-set will be demonstrated in many ways.

They Will Be Lovers of Money

Few words better describe the dominant idol in America than materialism. And, tragically, in God's eyes, materialism is also the dominant idol within the church. Jesus teaches, "For where your treasure is, there your heart will be also" (Matt. 6:21). In other words, our checkbooks and bank accounts reveal our hearts. For most in our churches, the checkbook reveals little or no heart for God because so many give little or nothing to their churches and/or Christian ministries. This is why Jesus said we have to choose between God and money (Matt. 6:24). He knew the number one competitor for our hearts is where we put our trust and find our security. For most people that trust and security is found in money and possessions rather than in God. Sadly, most in the church who profess to be Christians have chosen to put their trust in their bank accounts and not in God.

They Will Be Boastful, Arrogant, and Conceited

Listen to the average politician bragging about what they will do or have done. Watch the multitude of star athletes who pound their chests after doing something good for all the world to see. These types of self-serving gestures in team sports would have been soundly condemned a few years ago. Today they are the norm. This me-centered approach is really scoffing at God, who has given every successful person and athlete the gifts they have.

They Will Disobey Their Parents

The fifth commandment of the Big Ten is a clear command to honor our parents. It is central to a wholesome and noble society. Yet disobedience of parents is both a parent's and child's responsibility. The only way a child learns this is from their parents. Parents who spoil a child certainly don't teach this. Those who are constantly rescuing their child from self-imposed negative consequences create entitled children who feel they can do whatever they want, including not respect their parents. It's a vicious cycle.

They Will Be Ungrateful, Unloving, and Unforgiving

These words certainly describe the person who is a lover of self.

They Will Consider Nothing Sacred

They have no interest in good. Listen to the humor of today. See what is mocked. The raunchier and more profane, the better it is in the world's eyes.

They Will Slander Others

They will be cruel. They will betray their friends. The press has always been a champion at slander. But historically, most, in the name of common decency, exercised some self-control. Not today. With social media, all restraints are off. Anyone at any time can have a public platform. Another form of slander is malicious gossip. In the New Testament it is called *diabolos*. It is also the Greek word used for the devil. A culture that lives like the devil results in people acting cruelly and slanderously toward one another. Amazingly, many evangelical Christians buy into this type of slander through the political leaders and the television and talk radio personalities they choose to follow.

They Will Have No Self-Control

Whether it is our loose tongues, our rants on social media, or our addictions to alcohol or drugs or sex or porn or violence, modern human beings are increasingly becoming out of control.

They Will Love Pleasure Rather than God

This really sums up the "lover of self" mind-set. Love of money and love of pleasure are the two bookends to the love-of-self culture. People with these priorities do not love God.

They Will Hold to a Form of Godliness, though They Deny Its Power

As we look at the character traits of humankind in the last days, many in the church—in a self-righteous, judgmental way—think it describes only those outside the church. Yet Paul, in writing to the young pastor Timothy, is describing those not only outside the church but also inside the church. When the church's values begin to reflect culture's values more than Christ, the church is filled with people who have a form of religion. This form of religion is not a real, trusting relationship in following Jesus. More and more, the church is filled with pro-sin clergy who teach that the Bible is wrong, including what it says about sexual immorality being evil and the exclusiveness of Jesus as the only way to God. This mind-set believes that only parts of God's Word are true. They think much of it is out of date and needs to be ignored.

This attitude results in more and more cultural Christians who know a lot of Christian jargon and have a lot of head knowledge about the faith, but total surrender to follow Christ and His teachings in His Word is foreign to them. They follow a "form" of Christianity that is empty and powerless. With the church's calling to be salt and light in the world, it is little wonder that moral chaos results.

When these character traits become the cultural norm, it creates a longing for someone or something to bring sanity and order out of the moral chaos. The Antichrist will appear to be just the man for the job. Amid chaos, humankind is always willing to give up freedom for security and power for order. The 2016 presidential race and the mind-set of some of the candidates was a testimony to this fact.

Much of the appeal of Islam in the modern world speaks to this desire. The Muslim world rightly points out the moral decadence of America and the West and offers its religious ideology as the solution. And sadly, many are deceived by the evil of this false religion, thinking it is good.

Yet one day, the world's moral chaos will be so decadent that one man—a very strong, charismatic leader—will appear on the world scene to offer himself as the solution to end the moral chaos. In desperation, the world will be willing to grant him unparalleled political power and might.

Combine moral chaos with the birth pangs Jesus teaches us about in Matthew 24:3–8—false messiahs, false prophets inside and outside the church, wars and rumors of wars, and an increase in the intensity and frequency of natural disasters—and there will be a longing for one man to reinstate order out of the turmoil.

The Global Village for Business

I believe there will be another huge reason the world will turn to one man for leadership. We live in a global village for business. In a press conference regarding the Trans-Pacific Partnership on August 2, 2016, President Obama remarked, "Globalization means that economies around the world are more integrated than ever. . . . It is here to stay."[4] If gas prices get too high because oil shipped from the Middle East or Russia goes sky high, then the economy everywhere suffers. Yet when oil prices drop because the supply is greater than the demand, oil-rich nations in the Middle East, Russia, Africa, and South America can all suffer. This leads their economies to tank, and they have less money to buy the products exported from the United States, Europe, or China. Yet oil is just one commodity in the global village of business. We saw this in the midst of the freefall in early 2016.

It just makes sense that one day in the future when the global village is suffering greatly, the world will be more open to turning to one man to bring order and hope out of the worldwide depression. This is what happened in Germany with the rise of Adolf Hitler. Germany was hit hard by the Great Depression of the 1930s that came on top of the country's disastrous defeat in World War I. Desperate for a political and economic savior who would make Germany great again, they turned to Hitler, who was more charismatic than any other man in the twentieth century. At first he appeared to do a lot of good for Germany, yet little did Germany and the world know that this devil-filled leader would cause all hell to break loose in Europe and the Western world.

Remember, Hitler is a foreshadowing of what the Antichrist will be on a global scale. At first he will appear to do a lot of good. His charisma and leadership gifts will cause the world to worshipfully follow him. Yet little will everyone know that he will be the devil incarnate, seeking to unify the world around himself for his glory, strength, and might. This man will have a power far greater than Hitler's—supernatural power. God's Word speaks about that.

Will you be one of those cultural Christians swept up in the excitement and hope that a certain charismatic leader is the answer to the earth's increasing instability? Or will your biblical and spiritual eyes be open to the horrific danger that lies ahead if the masses put their trust in a political world leader who is not Jesus?

8

A Fatal Wound Is Healed

The Supernatural Power of the Antichrist

Just as the devil had Adolf Hitler poised and ready to seize power in Germany in the 1930s, so it will be when the Antichrist appears on the world scene. It will be the right timing and place for the events to unfold. Yet, what will set him apart from all the other Antichrist-type figures before him will be supernatural power:

> I saw one of his heads as if it had been slain, and his fatal wound was healed. And the whole earth was amazed and followed after the beast; they worshiped the dragon because he gave his authority to the beast; and they worshiped the beast, saying, "Who is like the beast, and who is able to wage war with him?" (Rev. 13:3–4)

God is not the only one with supernatural power. The devil has supernatural power as well. This makes perfect sense, for the Antichrist is the counterfeit Christ. Christ died on the cross. He rose from the dead. No miracle is greater than a man who is fully dead coming back to life. So it makes perfect sense that the counterfeit Christ would be empowered to counterfeit Jesus's death and resurrection.

The way Revelation 13:3 is written makes it appear that the Antichrist will be assassinated and killed, and then will miraculously come back to life. It implies that he won't really be dead as Jesus was. But the world and its admiring press will believe he has miraculously risen from the dead.

Because most people believe that only God has supernatural powers, the world will see his power to overcome death as being from God. In the world's eyes, the Antichrist will be extraordinarily blessed by God, and thus he will be seen as the one man who can unite the world and rescue it from chaos.

We live in a world of 24/7 news cycles. Pictures of the assassination of this up-and-coming leader will be seen on every news outlet and on the internet. Then later, when he has miraculously beaten death, the whole world will be in awe.

"There is no man like this man."

"He must be the man for this age."

"God's hand is upon him."

The only major group of people who will not believe these things will be followers of Christ who know and believe the Bible. This will increase the hostility and persecution of Christians in the world. Any questions raised about the "goodness" of the Antichrist by Christians will be met with almost universal hostility and contempt.

Peace in the Middle East?

Once the Antichrist begins to seize power, doesn't it make sense in the name of world unity and peace that his attention will turn to the powder keg of the Middle East? If he can bring about peace in the Middle East, he will be able to do what no man has ever done. It will be the diplomatic coup of the ages.

For a thoughtful examination of end times biblical prophecy, we turn again to the book of Daniel. For those unfamiliar with this book, its first six chapters contain historical events and miracles that inspire a believer's faith. Its biblical prophecy is simple to understand. The second half of Daniel, chapters 7–12, is a much more difficult biblical prophecy to grasp.

What is so amazing about Daniel's life is that he served as a powerful and trusted counselor to pagan kings of Babylon (Iraq) and then near the end of his life, under pagan kings of Persia (Iran) who had conquered Babylon. Yet after all his years in captivity, what he longed for in his long prayer in Daniel 9:1–19 was the restoration of Jerusalem for the Jewish people. Daniel confessed humbly and honestly how God's punishment on Israel had been deserved, for they had turned away from God and refused to repent.

The prayer is a masterpiece of the right spirit of a great spiritual leader humbly interceding on behalf of the sinful people God loves. His prayer is one every Christian leader ought to pray for the wayward, sin-riddled church in America today—a church that often seems like ancient Israel.

Once Daniel completes his prayer, the angel Gabriel comes and gives him a new prophetic vision that is recorded in Daniel 9:24–27:

Seventy weeks have been decreed for your people and your holy city, to finish the transgression, to make an end of sin, to make atonement for iniquity, to bring in everlasting righteousness, to seal up vision and prophecy and to anoint the most holy place. So you are to know and discern that from the issuing of a decree to restore and rebuild Jerusalem until Messiah the Prince there will be seven weeks and sixty-two weeks; it will be built again, with plaza and moat, even in times of distress. Then after the sixty-two weeks the Messiah will be cut off and have nothing, and the people of the prince who is to come will destroy the city and the sanctuary. And its end will come with a flood; even to the end there will be war; desolations are determined. And he will make a firm covenant with the many for one week, but in the middle of the week he will put a stop to sacrifice and grain offering; and on the wing of abominations will come one who makes desolate, even until a complete destruction, one that is decreed, is poured out on the one who makes desolate.

Michael Youssef writes in his book on Daniel that "biblical scholars are nearly unanimous in their agreement that this prophecy [in v. 24] refers to seventy sets of seven years." He then shares a fascinating study of how Jesus would be crucified on the exact day Daniel prophesied in verses 24–26.[1]

Let's focus on verse 27 and unpack it by first giving an interpretive version of the first half of it: "And he" (the Antichrist—if the "he" were the Messiah, it would be capitalized) "will make a firm covenant" (that's a sacred contract—a firm, legally binding commitment) "with the many" (Israel) "for one week" (seven years).

This verse tells us that the Antichrist will make some sort of peace treaty with Israel for seven years. That means he will have extraordinary power, influence, and diplomatic savvy to do so. Israel is surrounded by Muslim Arab nations that have sought to destroy the nation since the day of its miraculous rebirth on May 14, 1948. On the very first day of its rebirth, Egypt, Jordan, Lebanon, Syria, and Iraq declared war on Israel and told the Arabs living in Israel (called Palestinians) to flee to neighboring Arab states while they "pushed the Jews into the sea."[2] They planned to destroy this new nation before it could ever get off the ground. It was a miracle of biblical proportions that the six to seven hundred thousand Jews with very limited and primitive weapons survived that war while being attacked and surrounded by five Arab Muslim nations of megamillions of people.

Yet after all these years of constantly fighting for survival, Jews in Israel desperately long for peace. There is an understandable war-weariness among the Jewish people of Israel today.

Think about it. In 1993—under the leadership of US President Bill Clinton—the prime minister of Israel, Yitzhak Rabin, and Yasser Arafat, leader of the Palestinian Liberation Organization (PLO), signed the Oslo Accords. It was astounding because the PLO's charter had called for the elimination of Israel. The world was inspired and thrilled. At last there was hope for peace in the Middle East. But the optimism and celebration were short-lived. Why should anyone have been surprised? Yasser Arafat was one of the most diabolical terrorists in modern history, yet the leaders of Israel were willing to trust him with the Oslo Accords. It doesn't make sense, but it shows the desperate longing of many secular Jews in Israel to finally have lasting peace.

If Israel will trust an evil, duplicitous terrorist like Yasser Arafat in hopes of peace, then it is easy to see how the naive, peace-loving Israelis, who are biblically illiterate, will be drawn to trust a far more gifted and charismatic man of worldwide stature like the Antichrist.

Temple Mount

What testifies to the brilliant charisma and diplomatic genius of the Antichrist, though, is revealed in Daniel 9:27b:

> But in the middle of the week he will put a stop to sacrifice and grain offering.

This means the temple of the Jews will have been rebuilt in Jerusalem, for Jews can only make sacrifices at the temple. That ended when Rome leveled the temple in AD 70. There is only one place the temple can be built—the Temple Mount, where the third holiest site of Islam stands today, the Dome of the Rock.

Photo credit: Austin Smith.

The reason Israel's government constantly seeks to quell interest that religious Jews have for rebuilding the temple is they know it would be World War III if the temple were to be rebuilt on the site where the Dome of the Rock is today.

The closest this came to happening was at the end of the Six-Day War in June 1967, when the Israeli Jews liberated Jerusalem from occupation—a period that went all the way back to the Romans of the first century. They were reclaiming the sacred city God had given their King David almost three thousand years earlier.

On that day, some Jewish soldiers climbed to the top of the Dome of the Rock and raised the Israeli flag, which contains the Star of David, claiming the spot for the Jews. The Army's chief rabbi, Shlomo Goren, called for the destruction of the Dome of the Rock that day.[3] Such a request was understandable, for in doing so the Jews could rebuild the temple. Every day Orthodox Jews at the Western Wall pray, "Oh, Lord, send us the Messiah" and "Oh, Lord, restore our temple." But why is the rebuilding of the temple so important? So that biblically ordained worship with sacrifices can be reinstituted according to the teaching of the Holy Scriptures.

What an adrenaline rush for Israeli soldiers and Orthodox Jews on that day in 1967! But it did not happen. The great Israeli general, Moshe Dayan, interceded and ordered for the Israeli flag to be taken down from the Dome of the Rock.[4] He did so because he feared that Israel's great victory in battle that day could lead to the destruction of Israel in World War III. To this day, that is the stance of the Israeli government led by secular Jews.

So when Daniel 9:27 tells us the Antichrist will sign a peace treaty with Israel and three and a half years later will put an end to sacrifice in the temple that does not exist, this is a prophecy that cannot be fulfilled unless the Antichrist will be a man of such extraordinary power and influence that the temple is rebuilt. Extraordinary is an understatement, knowing the outrage in the Muslim world if that were to occur today.

But there is more. Daniel 9:27c tells us "and on the wing of abominations will come one who makes desolate, even until a complete destruction, one that is decreed, is poured out on the one who makes desolate."

What is this "abomination" that makes desolate? Timewise it will occur in the middle of the seven-year peace treaty with Israel. It is something so horrific that Jesus spoke about it:

> Therefore when you see the ABOMINATION OF DESOLATION which was spoken of through Daniel the prophet, standing in the holy place (let the reader understand). (Matt. 24:15)

Before we look at the answer to what exactly it is that Jesus calls the Abomination of Desolation, take a moment to consider how the stage is being set for a charismatic, brilliant world leader to enter the world scene. Think about the worship and aura around this man who seems to be so supernaturally blessed by God to come back from the dead and even bring peace to the Middle East. Consider a man so gifted and powerful that he can convince Muslims to allow Israel to rebuild the temple on the Temple Mount. Is it any wonder that the whole world will live in worshipful awe of this man? All this will set the stage for what Jesus and Daniel call the Abomination of Desolation. So what is it?

9

A Seat in the Temple of God

The Abomination of Desolation

Before we look at the Abomination of Desolation, think about what abomination means. It means unlawful; deceivers who "profess to know God, but by their deeds they deny Him" (Titus 1:16). I can't help but think about the pro-sin clergy who teach their churches that what God's Word says is an abomination is really something good (Lev. 18:22 and Deut. 22:5). The seven deadly sins in Proverbs 6:16–19—so common in the contemporary church and culture—are called an "abomination" to the Lord.

There is also one other word that defines the word *abomination*. It is *disgust*. These things are disgusting to the Lord. So when God calls something an abomination, He is speaking of sin and evil that are disgusting to Him.

Now let's go back to the Abomination of Desolation that both Daniel and Jesus prophesied.

Daniel's Prophecy

First, we have to make sense of Daniel's writing of the Antichrist stopping sacrifices in the temple three and a half years after he negotiates a peace treaty with Israel that would promise his power and might to the nation to protect them—a nation surrounded by hundreds of millions of Arab Muslims who want it eliminated. In the Arab-Muslim mind, Jerusalem and the land of Israel became Allah's land when they conquered it in AD 637. They made an emphatic statement about that in AD 692 with the building of the Dome of the Rock on the site of the Temple Mount where the ancient Jewish temple once stood. They felt this showed the world that Allah is superior to the Jewish God. Muslims reinforced that view with the building of the Al-Aqsa Mosque in AD 715. Today the Temple Mount, Dome of the Rock, and Al-Aqsa Mosque make Jerusalem the third holiest city in Islam after Mecca and Medina.

The Dome of the Rock is a shrine located on the site that Mohammed supposedly had his famous nocturnal journey to heaven. Al-Aqsa Mosque is where Muslims gather to this day for worship and prayer. So from a rational human perspective, there is no way the Jewish temple could be rebuilt on that site. The secular Israeli government monitors any movement of Bible-believing Jews who want to see the Dome of the Rock torn down for the rebuilding of the Jewish temple. In addition to this, Orthodox Jews mostly believe that the temple will not be rebuilt until the Messiah comes.

So how could Daniel's prophecy speak of the Antichrist putting a stop to the sacrifices in Daniel 9:27? The only place Jews can make sacrifices is the temple in Jerusalem. But there is no temple. The chances of its being rebuilt are nil. Israel would face the wrath of the whole Muslim world. It would be a desecration of the third holiest site of Islam. Plus, knowing the growing anti-Semitism in places like Europe, Russia, and Central Asia, it would be suicidal for Israel to do so.

So how in the world can this prophecy come about? This takes us to the new covenant found in 2 Thessalonians 2:1–2:

> Now we request you, brethren, with regard to the coming of our Lord Jesus Christ and our gathering together to Him, that you not be quickly shaken from your composure or be disturbed either by a spirit or a message or a letter as if from us, to the effect that the day of the Lord has come.

The church at Thessalonica was continually worried that they may have missed the second coming of Jesus. Paul wrote verse 1 to reassure them that they had not. Then he went on to write about certain events that will occur before Jesus comes again:

> Let no one in any way deceive you, for it will not come unless the apostasy comes first. (2 Thess. 2:3a)

What is "the apostasy"? Apostasy is the falling away of Christians from God. It is the falling away of churches from God. In America and Europe, we have seen the falling away of whole denominations from God. Europe led the way in this with its rationalist approach to Scripture in the twentieth century. That approach essentially rejected the sacred authority of Scripture as God's Word. Sadly, in many Protestant denominations in Europe, we saw a falling away. This is ironic because Protestant theology was founded on Martin Luther's premise of *sola scriptura* (Scripture alone is the authority for the belief and practice of our faith).

From Protestant Theologians to Powerless Pulpits to Empty Pews

Today many great cathedrals of Europe are empty places of worship except for the thousands of tourists who come to admire the Gothic architecture of days gone by. The theology of the authority of the church and Scripture have not always been watered down, but the European culture as a whole no longer sees the church as relevant to everyday life. For hundreds and hundreds and hundreds of years, Europe was the stronghold of Christianity. Today it is seen as a relic of the past, a giant reminder of the apostasy of the church.

In the 1950s and 1960s, mainline Protestant leaders in America began to follow the direction of the European church and diminish the trustworthiness of Scripture as the authoritative Word of God. The liberal clergy began to embrace contemporary values of culture over the teaching of God's Word. Universalism, the idea that all people of all faiths can get to God and heaven in their own ways, became dominant. This of course completely ignores the teaching of Jesus, who said, "I am the way, and the truth, and the life; no one comes to the Father but through Me" (John 14:6). Sadly, because many mainline Protestant denominations have embraced universalism and the idolatry of political correctness over Scripture, the apostasy of the church is the result.

Even more sad to me is the number of evangelical Christians who have become practical Universalists. Many really don't believe their nice neighbors and co-workers without Jesus are headed to hell. One leading evangelical megachurch pastor named Rob Bell wrote a bestselling book, *Love Wins*, based on that idea. Now he is out of the pastorate and teaching with the leading American guru of universalism, Oprah Winfrey. Sadly, she may be America's most influential spiritual leader.

Other evangelical Christians are embracing politically correct views of sexuality that villainize what Scripture says is good concerning sexual purity. Added to that are the many "health and wealth gospel" churches, that often claim to believe the Bible as authoritatively true but espouse a heresy that could really be called the "gospel of greed." Jesus taught just the opposite.

Apostasy is growing rapidly in the American church, and health and wealth heresy is exploding with followers in the fast-growing Christian churches in Africa, especially in Nigeria. Apostasy of the church is continually before our eyes, and the apostle Paul writes that it must come first before Jesus comes again.

He writes of another important development:

And the man of lawlessness is revealed, the son of destruction. (2 Thess. 2:3b)

This is the Antichrist. Although he is the embodiment of evil—the devil in the flesh—he will appear on the world's scene as a man of good, a man for world unity and peace. Look at what he will do:

[He] opposes and exalts himself above every so-called god or object of worship, so that he takes his seat in the temple of God, displaying himself as being God. (2 Thess. 2:4)

Remember, there is no temple. To rebuild it would surely lead to World War III and the destruction of Israel at the hands of the Muslim world and an increasingly anti-Semitic world. Yet Daniel prophesied that the Antichrist will negotiate a peace treaty with Israel and in the middle of it—after three and a half years—he will stop the sacrifices in the temple.

Obviously, both Daniel and 2 Thessalonians are telling us that the temple will be rebuilt. When it is, sacrifices will be resumed.

Then at some point the Antichrist will enter the rebuilt temple and declare himself God. This will reveal his true heart, for world peace and unity is to be centered on worship of him as God. All through history this has been the mindset of Antichrist-types such as Nebuchadnezzar of Babylon, Alexander the Great of Greece, the Caesars of Rome, or in the modern age, Adolf Hitler. Although Hitler didn't claim to be God, he acted as if he were to be worshiped as the great all-powerful ruler of Europe. Incredibly, the most cultured and sophisticated culture of Europe, Germany, bought into his incredible passion and charisma and believed it.

Can one man one day do in the world what Hitler tried to do in Europe? Scripture says emphatically *yes*!

And nothing will bolster the Antichrist as a man of supernatural diplomatic skills more than him allowing for the rebuilding of the temple. It will be the ultimate diplomatic coup of history. But how can this occur on the sacred Muslim site of the Dome of the Rock? How could he ever get the 1.7 billion Muslims of the world to agree? They have claimed that land for Allah. It is a sacred spot. Only a person of supernatural skills in diplomacy and charisma and power could think of pulling this off. Only an incredible leader—so charming, so persuasive, so powerful.

That man is the Antichrist.

When it occurs, the world will be in awe. There will be such a sense of wonder at his greatness and charisma that the worship of Hitler in Nazi Germany will seem miniscule compared to the worship of the Antichrist.

So how will he do it?

Many scholars believe that the ancient Jewish temple was behind the Eastern Gate, a gate that is now sealed. It is the gate through which the Messiah will enter Jerusalem to begin His reign from the throne of David after he touches down on the Mount of Olives.

There is plenty of room behind the Eastern Gate to rebuild the Jewish temple without harming the Dome of the Rock. Both sacred sites could stand side by side. What would be a greater testimony to world peace and unity espoused by the Antichrist than these two great religions (so long at odds) now sharing a sacred site?

How he will convince the Muslim world to do this, I do not know. Some believe that Ezekiel 38–39 explains this when it says Gog and Magog (a confederation of nations, led by Russia, that includes some Muslim nations like Iran) will be destroyed when they invade Israel. God will destroy their attacking armies by bringing a great earthquake and fire and brimstone from heaven (Ezek. 38:18–19).[1] During that earthquake, maybe the Dome of the Rock and Al-Aqsa will be destroyed. I am skeptical of this because I believe what Ezekiel was describing occurs one thousand years from

Jesus's second coming (Rev. 20:7–10). We really do not know, but somehow the Antichrist will pull this off since he will have somehow convinced Israel to sign the peace treaty that guarantees their protection (Dan. 9:27). Then Israel will be thrilled. Remember, Israel is composed of mostly secular Jews who desperately long for peace. And although most Orthodox Jews believe the Messiah will be the man to rebuild the temple, the promise of the rebuilt temple and renewal of sacrifices will be more than they can resist. They will see it as a long-awaited answer to their daily prayers.

Doesn't it make sense that if the Antichrist pulls off this astounding achievement, then he would want to come and celebrate his diplomatic genius? Maybe it will be an official ceremony with leaders from the United Nations from around the world. Every news outlet in every nation will be covering the historic events of Muslim imams and Jewish rabbis gathered together on the Temple Mount in mutual respect. All the world will feel that there is—at last—peace in the Middle East. What a joyful celebration it will be.

Then doesn't it make sense that the Antichrist will see this as the perfect opportunity to enter the Jewish temple and declare himself God? He will be "the one" to be worshiped for bringing about world unity and peace. Because the world will be so spiritually lost, people will scream, "*Yes!* He is the great one! All hail, man of peace."

God's Word tells us this:

> They worshiped the dragon because he gave his authority to the beast; and they worshiped the beast, saying, "Who is like the beast, and who is able to wage war with him?" There was given to him a mouth speaking arrogant words and blasphemies, and authority to act for forty-two months

was given to him. And he opened his mouth in blasphemies against God, to blaspheme His name and His tabernacle, that is, those who dwell in heaven. (Rev. 13:4–6)

Yet when he does this, those who have come to faith in Christ will not be surprised. But one group will be stunned and horrified—the Jews of Israel. Yes, the overwhelming number of Jews in Israel today are not religious, but one thing even secular Jews will realize (and Orthodox Jews firmly believe) is that there is only one God—Yahweh. This was the major reason the majority of Jews rejected Jesus in His ministry on earth more than two thousand years ago. He claimed to be the Son of God. "Blasphemy," they said. And they schemed with the Roman authorities to have Him crucified for blasphemy—the worst of sins.

So in this day when the Antichrist enters the rebuilt temple and shockingly declares himself God, the Jews of Israel will realize they have made a deal with the devil. They will be horrified. They will be appalled. They will rebel against him.

This will outrage the world against them. But most of all, it will outrage the Antichrist. He will respond like any megalomaniac Antichrist-type figure. He will be furious. Doesn't it make sense that the first thing he orders will be a stop to sacrifices to the Jewish God? And that will be only the beginning of his fury against Israel. All hell will break loose in Israel (and the world) for the next three and a half years.

Many biblical Jews will remember the words of the prophet Daniel in Daniel 9:27: "And on the wing of abominations will come one who makes desolate, even until a complete destruction, one that is decreed, is poured out on the one who makes desolate."

The Abomination of Desolation will have come.

10

A Nightmare Unfolds

The Great Tribulation Unleashed on the Earth

When I lead Bible study tours to Israel, it is fascinating to see the rubble of giant stones at the southern base of the Western Wall. It is a visible testimony to the fulfillment of Jesus's prophecy:

> Jesus came out from the temple and was going away when His disciples came up to point out the temple buildings to Him. And He said to them, "Do you not see all these things? Truly I say to you, not one stone here will be left upon another, which will not be torn down." (Matt. 24:1–2)

There have been three times in history when an Abomination of Desolation of God's holy place in the temple has been desecrated.

1. The first time occurred in the sixth century BC when Nebuchadnezzar was king of Babylon. He was the most

powerful man in all the world, for the Babylonians were the most powerful kingdom. Nebuchadnezzar brought Jerusalem under siege and eventually destroyed the majestic temple Solomon had built in 587 BC. He also took many Jews to Babylon in one of the darkest days of Jewish history—the Babylonian captivity.

Eventually, Cyrus the Great of Persia (modern-day Iran) conquered Babylon and let the Jews return to their homeland and even rebuild their temple. (If you want to read prophecy that will astound you, just read Isaiah 44:28–45:6, which explains how Isaiah was led by the Holy Spirit to prophesy this almost two hundred years before there ever was a Cyrus the Great. Amazing!)

2. The second desecration of the temple occurred in 168 BC when the rebuilt temple was desecrated by Antiochus Epiphanes, the Greek king of the Seleucids. He conquered Jerusalem and desecrated the temple by building an altar to Zeus, the mythological god of Greece. Then to add insult to injury, he sacrificed pigs on the altar. Jews consider pigs to be the filthiest of unclean animals. This was truly an Abomination of Desolation to the Jews.

3. The third time an Abomination of Desolation occurred was the time Jesus prophesied in Matthew 24:1–2, as stated above. It occurred in AD 70 when the Romans, under Titus, destroyed the rebuilt temple.

Yet none of these events are the events mentioned in Daniel 9:27 and Matthew 24:15. Daniel writes of a day when the Antichrist will put an end to sacrifice in the rebuilt temple. Second Thessalonians 2:4 fills in the details—that it will be an Abomination of Desolation when the Antichrist enters the temple and declares himself God.

When Jesus spoke of this, He warned Jews of Israel that they will need to "run for the hills," for all hell will be about to break loose in Israel:

> Therefore when you see the ABOMINATION OF DESOLATION which was spoken of through Daniel the prophet, standing in the holy place (let the reader understand), then those who are in Judea must flee to the mountains. Whoever is on the housetop must not go down to get the things out that are in his house. Whoever is in the field must not turn back to get his cloak. But woe to those who are pregnant and to those who are nursing babies in those days! But pray that your flight will not be in the winter, or on a Sabbath. For then there will be a great tribulation, such as has not occurred since the beginning of the world until now, nor ever will. (Matt. 24:15–21)

Some argue that Jesus's prophecy of the destruction of the temple in Matthew 24:1–2 was fulfilled in AD 70 by the Romans and was also the Abomination of Desolation He spoke of. Yet there was no way Jews could have headed for the hills, for the Romans had all Jerusalem under siege. On top of that, in Matthew 24:21 Jesus prophesied that when the Abomination of Desolation occurs there will be a "great tribulation, such as has not occurred since the beginning of the world until now, nor ever will." That certainly didn't happen when Rome destroyed the temple in AD 70.

Daniel 12:11 tells us the Great Tribulation period will be 1,290 days. That's 3.5 years, plus 30 days. Revelation 13:4–5 tells us that the Antichrist will reign over this period of forty-two months (3.5 years).

Revelation 6–18 describes the Great Tribulation. It is not a pretty picture. *Warning*: Don't read Revelation 6–18 before you go to bed at night. You won't be able to sleep well. You are liable to have nightmares. It paints a horrid picture of all hell breaking loose in the heavens and the earth. No one in their right mind will want to be around in those days. Plagues, famines, death, terror, reigns of blood, and asteroids pounding the earth will be so bad that according to Jesus, "Unless those days had been cut short, no life would have been saved; but for the sake of the elect those days will be cut short" (Matt. 24:22).

The elect are the true followers of Jesus. They will not be forgotten. They are those who come to Christ in the Great Tribulation.

In Revelation 13:1–2, the Antichrist (the beast) is introduced onto the world scene. The Antichrist will appear to have been mortally wounded and yet will somehow survive (Rev. 13:3). This will cause the world to worship him (v. 4), because they will think he has risen from the dead. He will reign for forty-two months after speaking blasphemies (claiming to be God), as he does when he enters the rebuilt temple of Jerusalem and declares himself God (vv. 5–6).

Revelation 13:7 then focuses on the Antichrist's hostility toward Christians:

> It was also given to him to make war with the saints and to overcome them, and authority over every tribe and people and tongue and nation was given to him.

Jesus called Christians "the elect" (Matt. 24:22, 24, 31; Mark 13:20, 22, 27; Luke 18:7). Verse 7 refers to Christians as "the saints." The majority of Christians will already have been rescued from this time through Christ rapturing His

104

church. Yet obviously after that occurs, some of those left behind will come to Christ. These are the saints mentioned in Revelation 13:7.

The Antichrist by this time will be ruling over a one-world government. But can one man rule the world? God's Word says one man will have that temporary authority. One-world governments have been the ambition of Antichrist-type rulers and the longing of many ideologies throughout history.

Fast-forward to the twentieth century, when Marxist ideology had this utopian vision of a one-world atheistic state through power and might. I remember visiting with a communist atheist government leader in China years ago and asking him to tell me the philosophy of communism. With an arrogant and sinister smile, he said, "We believe that power resides in the barrel of a gun." I felt a shiver go up my spine at the true methodology of communism's utopian agenda so honestly described.

Beginning in the twentieth century, Europe began to long for a one-world government—not by military might and power, but by a man-made ideology called political correctness. It continues to this day, with many in the United States following Europe's example. Now, in the twenty-first century, all the world is seeing this utopian goal of Islam that goes all the way back to the seventh century AD—one-world government under submission to Allah through Sharia law, the body of Islamic law. ISIS (ISIL) is the latest branch of Islam to espouse this longing.

Interestingly, some of the intellectual elite of America— mostly on the West and East Coasts—are really more "internationalists" than patriotic Americans. Internationalists rarely verbalize this, but they long to see the United Nations as more authoritative than the US government. They see themselves more as citizens of planet Earth than citizens of America. Even though President Obama would probably deny it, many statements he has made reveal he is more of an internationalist than a traditional American president.

Yet as idealistic as many may be with one-world utopian dreams, if we have a one-world government, somebody has to lead it. That presents a real problem. Lord Acton once said, "Absolute power corrupts absolutely."[1] This is true because of humankind's sinfulness. We all need checks and balances. This is why America's Founding Fathers wrote checks and balances into the executive and legislative and judicial branches of government. They were not blind to humankind's sin. One man with unchecked power (King George III of Great Britain) led to the American Revolution. Well, imagine one man with unchecked power over all the world. That is the devil incarnate. It will not be a pretty sight for anyone who opposes him.

Additionally, he will have a great advocate, enforcer, and cheerleader who will constantly work to see that all the world follows and worships him. That advocate is called the false prophet. His role will be to make the whole world fall in line under the leadership of the "great one," the Antichrist. The stage being set continues.

11

The Demonic Trinity Revealed

The False Prophet and the Mark of the Beast

Then I saw another beast coming up out of the earth; and he had two horns like a lamb and he spoke as a dragon. He exercises all the authority of the first beast in his presence. And he makes the earth and those who dwell in it to worship the first beast, whose fatal wound was healed. (Rev. 13:11–12)

The False Prophet

Who is the second beast? If the dragon is the devil and the beast is the Antichrist, then who is this second beast—a terrifying, animal-like evil being? It is the false prophet.

Now the demonic trinity is coming into focus. The Bible teaches us that we believe in a triune God—one God in three persons. He is the Father and the Son and the Holy Spirit. The Son, Jesus, is God in the flesh—totally submissive to His

Father's will. The Holy Spirit convicts us of our sinfulness and need for a Savior. Once we receive Jesus as Savior and Lord, the Holy Spirit dwells within us to point us to Jesus Christ. The Holy Spirit doesn't desire to call attention to Himself but that we might worship Jesus as Lord.

The devil wants to usurp God, which is why he, as an angel, led a rebellion against God in heaven. Revelation 12:8–9 tells of how God cast the devil and his angelic followers (demons) out of heaven. The Antichrist is the counterfeit Christ. Just as Jesus is God in the flesh, the Antichrist is the devil in a man. And just as the Holy Spirit points people to worship and follow Christ as Lord, the false prophet is the devil's counterfeit to the Holy Spirit (and to John the Baptist as well). The false prophet's goal is to have everyone on the earth worship the Antichrist, who will supposedly be fatally wounded and come back to life (the devil's counterfeit to Jesus's death and resurrection).

The false prophet, being filled with the devil, will have supernatural power like the devil. He, like the Antichrist, will appear to be good—even gentle like a lamb—when he appears on the world scene. "Like a lamb" are the words Scripture uses to describe Jesus. Oh, how the devil seeks to counterfeit in every way! Many believe he will be a key religious leader, for he will focus on the supernatural more than the Antichrist, who will be known for his extraordinary skills and charisma as a political leader. As Joseph Goebbels was for Hitler—seeking to center all the attention and Nazi propaganda on the greatness of the führer—so will the false prophet be for the Antichrist.

The false prophet will deceive the people of the earth with supernatural signs.

He Will Call Down Fire from Heaven

He performs great signs, so that he even makes fire come down out of heaven to the earth in the presence of men. (Rev. 13:13)

Just as God sent fire and brimstone from heaven on Sodom and Gomorrah (when the sin of homosexuality and sexual pleasure had engulfed those two cities), so will the false prophet counterfeit that power. Just as Elijah called down fire from heaven in his showdown with the false prophets of Baal, so will the false prophet counterfeit God's power. People will be amazed. The cultural Christians who know those biblical stories will be easily fooled into thinking that this false prophet and Antichrist must be empowered by God because only God can do that. It is also a reminder of why many members of almost every church will be around to keep the machinery of the church running after the true Christians have been raptured—because so many within America's churches are cultural Christians.

He Will Call for an Image of the Beast to Be Built and Worshiped

And he deceives those who dwell on the earth because of the signs which it was given him to perform in the presence of the beast, telling those who dwell on the earth to make an image to the beast who had the wound of the sword and has come to life. And it was given to him to give breath to the image of the beast, so that the image of the beast would even speak and cause as many as do not worship the image of the beast to be killed. (Rev. 13:14–15)

Amazingly, supernaturally, "the image" will be given breath so it can speak. I have no idea in our technologically sophisticated world how the Antichrist will do this. It sounds as goofy and hokey as the Wizard of Oz. Yet it will be seriously real and deadly serious for those who do not bow down. They will be killed.

In reading Bradley Martin's book *Under the Loving Care of the Fatherly Leader: North Korea and the Kim Dynasty*, I was sickened to learn of the viciously cruel reign over the North Korean people. It is the closest thing today to what will happen in the day of the Antichrist. Any North Korean citizen who does not bow to a giant statue of Kim Il-Sung, the founder of North Korea, or bow to his heirs, Kim Jong-il and today Kim Jong-un, faces death.

It makes one shudder to know that in those days the whole world will be in the satanic grip of the Antichrist like North Korea is with the Kims today.

The Mark of the Beast

> And he causes all, the small and the great, and the rich and the poor, and the free men and the slaves, to be given a mark on their right hand or on their forehead, and he provides that no one will be able to buy or to sell, except the one who has the mark, either the name of the beast or the number of his name. (Rev. 13:16–17)

Then the false prophet will devise a loyalty oath to the Antichrist that will be a matter of life and death to the world's citizens. Those loyal to the Antichrist will be given a mark on their foreheads or wrists. It will be sold as the latest in modern technology. No more need for drivers' licenses, credit cards, and checkbooks, for it will all be shrewdly tied into economics. No one will be able to buy or sell in the world economic system without this mark of the beast.

It caused me to gulp when I pulled the September 10, 2014, issue of *Time* magazine out of my mailbox. The cover story pictured the new Apple Watch.

It told how great it was going to be—just like strapping a mini-computer onto your wrist. It was called the "always there" internet. It tracks your movement—kind of like the GPS devices in our cars and the smartphones we carry. It puts your whole body online. A user can even pay for goods and services with it. Credit cards will not be needed anymore. But what really caught my attention was the article stating, "Once you're OK with wearing technology, the only way forward is inward; the next product launch after the Apple Watch would logically be the iMplant."[1]

I thought about the mob scenes in Apple stores when the latest product is introduced. Today no company is worth more than Apple. There is nothing bad about that, but just think what will happen when all this inevitable modern technology gets in the wrong hands—like the hands of an all-powerful, one-world government led by a dictator who is the devil incarnate.

Google advertises that it can accommodate the transactions of more than four trillion messages. The company's satellites show us pictures of all our neighborhoods—our individual homes—taken at such close range that we can recognize them.

The National Security Agency (NSA) of America's federal government began tracking our phone calls by the millions in the aftermath of 9/11. They did this with the good intentions of protecting us from Islamic terrorism and tracking foreign intelligence. But what if this technology falls into evil hands?

On February 25, 2002, abcnews.com published an article titled, "Implant Chip, Track People." It talks about how wonderful it will be as parents for our teenagers to have implanted chips in their wrists so we can know where they are at any time. The article reports how the company, Applied Digital Systems, in Palm Beach, Florida, has applied to the FDA for permission to test their VeriChip product in humans. Just the size of a grain of rice.[2] No problem. We already do this with pets.

The technology is here. Revelation 13:16–17 could become a reality when the Antichrist and his false prophet enter the world scene. Obviously, with the global economy and centralized government tracking technology, it is imminent that this prophecy in God's Word will be fulfilled.

Yet one big mystery has not been revealed:

> Here is wisdom. Let him who has understanding calculate the number of the beast, for the number is that of a man; and his number is six hundred and sixty-six. (Rev. 13:18)

Who is this? What does it symbolize? It symbolizes the Antichrist. His mark will be symbolized by the number 666.

People through the ages have speculated as to whom this is. We simply do not know. But what we do know is that when the Antichrist enters the world scene, empowered by the devil himself and promoted by the false prophet, all the world will know what 666 is.

How shrewd of the devil to pick a plan that will determine people's inclusion or rejection in the world's financial system. No mark—no money. No mark—no bank account.

No mark—no ability to buy and sell. Initially, it will just all make sense. It will simplify everyone's life. No cash, no checks, no credit cards needed. It will all be so convenient with the added "cool" of the latest technology.

Yet Jesus tells us in the greatest sermon ever preached that we must choose between God and money. He did this because he knew the greatest competitor for most people's hearts is money. It is where most people put their trust and find their security. It is why Jesus said, "Where your treasure is, there your heart will be" (Matt. 6:21).

In our churches, members tell God where their hearts are by their checkbooks. Most give little or nothing to God. The overwhelming majority do not even tithe, which is God's starting point in faithful giving. The tithe says to God, "I trust you with all I have." When we do or don't tithe, it screams volumes about where our hearts are. Those same cultural Christians who fill every church's pews will still be around when the Antichrist and false prophet make it clear that everyone must worship and submit to the Antichrist. If they do not, they will be left out of the economic system. If you're one of those "so-called Christians" still around, what will you decide? The answer is easy. Since most people in America's churches have already made the decision to choose money over God (and their checkbooks reveal it), it will be an easy decision for those left behind to make.

There will be no doubt that most will choose the mark of the beast, for they declare to God every week, every month, every year, that when it comes to choosing God or money, they have chosen to put their trust in their money rather than God.

Are You a Cultural Christian?

If you are one of those cultural Christians whose checkbook reveals to Jesus that you are not really His, isn't it best for you to get this right? The Bible has an old-fashioned word for it—repent. Change your mind in a way that changes your actions to be in tune with God's will. That's what repentance is. Scripture repeatedly challenges us to repent and put our trust in Jesus.

If you don't get it right now, when the choice can be disguised from everyone except God, why do you think you'll act any differently when the Antichrist forces you to make your allegiance known? I hope you'll decide to change your mind and put your trust in Jesus as your Savior and Lord. When you do, you will want your bank account to be a testimony that your heart is with Jesus.

12

Evil Unrestrained

How the World Will Be Deceived

The Antichrist will come to power with extraordinary gifts of leadership. Yet the question still arises: If he is the devil incarnate, appearing to be good when he is really evil in the flesh, how can the majority of the world not notice?

Well, in 2 Thessalonians 2:1–4, the apostle Paul assured the Thessalonian Christians that Jesus had not yet come because the apostasy of the church comes first. Second, the temple will miraculously be rebuilt where the Antichrist will enter and declare himself God, wanting to unify the world around himself. So how will all the world be deceived? Second Thessalonians 2:5–7 gives us major insight:

> Do you not remember that while I was still with you, I was telling you these things? And you know what restrains him now, so that in his time he will be revealed. For the mystery

of lawlessness is already at work; only he who now restrains will do so until he is taken out of the way.

The Antichrist will be restrained until "he who now restrains . . . is taken out of the way" (v. 7). What is restraining the Antichrist? Who is restraining him?

Some suggest it is national governments. The key reason God has ordained government as an important worldly institution is to uphold justice, protect the citizens from within and without, and punish evil (Rom. 13:1–4). Yet government is often the embodiment of evil. Look at the Babylonian and Assyrian Empires. Consider the twentieth century with Hitler's Nazi Germany, Stalin's Soviet Union, and Mao's China. All these governments killed megamillions of their own citizens. Today North Korea's Kim cult government is truly the embodiment of pure evil—not to mention Iran's government, along with ISIL, Hezbollah, Hamas, and Somalia's Muslim-led regimes that are the embodiment of ruthless Islamic terrorism.

So if government is not the restrainer, what is?

The restrainer is the Holy Spirit, and the Holy Spirit resides in individual Christians and thus Christ's church. When we come to trust Christ as Savior and Lord, we are given the gift of the Holy Spirit. There is no separate baptism of the Holy Spirit. We are baptized with the Holy Spirit the moment we are spiritually born into the kingdom of God through repentant faith in Christ.

Once the restrainer—the Holy Spirit, dwelling in believers in Christ (the church)—is removed from the world's scene, there is no longer a restraint on evil. This is why Jesus said in the Sermon on the Mount that Christians are to be salt and light in this world (Matt. 5:13–16).

Salt adds taste to food when used properly. But salt in the ancient world was used to prevent meat from decaying. My grandfather had many different jobs before he was called into full-time vocational ministry in his thirties. He had been mayor of the small town he lived in. He had run a grocery store. There he learned from the butchers how to cure meat. He had a personal interest in this because he loved country ham. So when I was a boy and we visited my grandfather's house, he would proudly show me the room off from the kitchen where he cured country ham—basically packed in salt—so the meat would be good for a long time. Salt is a preservative.

People without Christ are spiritually dead. One of the roles of Christians and the church is to be the spiritual and moral preservative in a spiritually dead world. When there is no more salt—no more church—the spiritual and moral decay occurs rapidly, and it is not a pretty picture.

Many Christians have asked me this question: How could America change so rapidly from being a culture that upholds the moral sanctity of marriage being between one man and one woman, to where it is today, with the majority embracing an unbiblical and immoral view of redefining marriage to include same-sex couples? The answer is pretty sobering. As the church has less and less influence (because the majority of our churches are filled with people who mirror culture more than look like Jesus in spirit and character), the restraint on spiritual and moral decay is removed. When this occurs, evil flourishes.

The church is also called to be light to a spiritually dark world. Jesus said He is the light of the world. When we begin to trust and follow Him, His light (the Holy Spirit) is to shine through us with the love and grace and good news of Christ.

Our light is to illuminate the truth—that is, Jesus—yet because so few of us Christians shine our lights as faithful and fruitful witnesses for Christ, the world becomes a darker and darker place.

The restraint on evil is lowered when the church mirrors culture more than it transforms culture, because it covers up the light that Jesus wants us to be.

Yet 2 Thessalonians 2:5–6 is not referring to the spiritual and moral compromise of the church and the cowardly fear of hiding the light of Christ from those around us today. It is speaking of how the Holy Spirit (through the church) is totally removed from the world's scene. When that occurs, the Antichrist will be revealed and quickly embraced by the world:

> Then that lawless one will be revealed whom the Lord will slay with the breath of His mouth and bring to an end by the appearance of His coming; that is, the one whose coming is in accord with the activity of Satan, with all power and signs and false wonders, and with all the deception of wickedness for those who perish, because they did not receive the love of the truth so as to be saved. (2 Thess. 2:8–10)

The Antichrist will be able to deceive the people of the world who have not received the truth (Jesus) to be saved (from death and hell). The result will be a deluding influence that descends on the people of the earth so they believe what is false. America is getting a taste of this as so many have begun to believe that what God teaches is evil is actually good. People are being deluded into believing what is false, for the salt of the church has lost its savor and the light of the church has been covered (Matt. 5:15-16).

In the Israeli-Hamas war in the summer of 2014, I was stunned to read that more millennials (Americans born from

1980 to 2000, the largest generation in American history) were supportive of Hamas than of Israel.[1] Hamas is a Muslim terrorist organization that publicly calls for the elimination of Israel, the only true democracy in the Middle East.

How could millennials support Hamas? It's simple. With the overwhelming number of millennials being ungrounded biblically and choosing not to be a Christian and part of the church, how could they know? We should not be surprised. A deluding influence sets in when there is less salt and light in the world.

When people have not received salvation through faith in Jesus, they become spiritually blind—to the truth and to evil—and wickedness results:

> In order that they all may be judged who did not believe the truth, but took pleasure in wickedness. (2 Thess. 2:12)

Sadly, in the end, judgment results. Judgment that leads to hell can be avoided when we trust Christ. God gives us a choice. Either we face judgment for our sins or we receive His grace through faith that Christ has paid the price of judgment for our sins. The choice is ours.

In the meantime, Christians and the church are still in the world. And though the church's influence in America and Europe has declined, it is growing dramatically in other parts of the world. The salt still preserves against decay. The light of Christ still shines. Yet one day, the salt and light of this world will be removed, and with no more restraint on evil, the Antichrist will be poised to be revealed and to rule.

So when will that occur? When will the church and Christians be removed from the world's scene? That is another key event leading up to the end of the age.

13

The Ultimate Destination Wedding

Jesus Returns for His Bride

Let's now shift our focus from the Antichrist and the time when all hell breaks loose to when the Holy Spirit is removed from the world scene. Is it before the Antichrist appears on the world scene? Is it while he is the dominant personality in the world? Or is it near the end of his power, before he is destroyed with a word by Jesus? Some even wonder if the church will be removed at all.

This leads us to the rapture of the church. Many say the idea of the rapture is a new theological idea that did not arise until the nineteenth century under the leadership of John Nelson Darby in the 1830s.[1]

Others speculated about it, like Puritan preachers Increase and Cotton Mather, but Darby popularized it. Because of this, many discredit it. When I began to see how clearly Scripture teaches the rapture, I had not studied Darby and had never even used the Scofield version of the Bible that had helped popularize it. I sure didn't come by this from my theological education. I went to a seminary that held a condescending view of evangelical Christians and continually mocked popular evangelical views of eschatology (end times).

That's the beauty of simply studying God's Word to understand what each passage means—it allows any Christian or preacher of the gospel to enter the study without preconceived notions. This allows the Holy Spirit to speak to us in the spirit of "the priesthood of the believer" that Martin Luther talked about in his call for reform in the sixteenth century. Commentaries of multiple theological and hermeneutical views then help us critically assess if we have misinterpreted the obvious or misunderstood the leading of the Holy Spirit.

So I write this out of a study that I began in preaching through the book of Revelation about twenty-five years ago. I'm ashamed to say that for the first ten years of pastoring, I stayed away from anything having to do with the book of Revelation, biblical prophecy, and the end times. I did this for two main reasons: (1) it seemed irrelevant to everyday life; and (2) I was intimidated by all the symbolism of Revelation that had led to a multitude of difficult and speculative interpretations. I feel many young pastors in the millennial generation feel the same way today. But after finally becoming convinced that this is an important part of God's Word, I moved forward with fear and trepidation.

Amazingly, Revelation came alive. I was enthralled and amazed. I finished that study realizing that yes, there are many different interpretations, but we can clearly understand many aspects of the events leading to Jesus's second coming.

Then my wife and I took our first Bible study tour to Israel. We were expecting a mostly biblical historical study involving going to sites of biblical events. It was certainly that, but what stunned us was seeing the biblical prophecy that is unfolding right before our eyes today in Israel. That began what has led to sixteen Bible study tours of Israel and a passionate fascination with biblical prophecy as perhaps the most relevant study of Scripture that applies to everyday life. When we understand biblical prophecy and see how world events are leading to the second coming of Christ, we watch and listen to daily news knowing we have been let in on a huge secret. None of these events are random. They are all part of God's sovereign plan for history. Yes, we don't know the details of how it will all unfold, but we do know where history is heading. Much of the big picture regarding significant news events of our world, especially in the Middle East, illuminates prophecy unfolding right before our eyes.

One conclusion I have come to in studying Revelation and biblical prophecy in the Old and New Testaments is that a rapture of the church will occur sometime before Jesus's second coming. I still have not read a thing that Darby wrote. I still have not seen the study material on this in the Scofield Bible.

Yet in studying Revelation, I came to realize that the definitive passage on the rapture is not 1 Thessalonians 4:13–17. That passage tells how it will happen. The definitive passage is Revelation 19:7–9. It describes the ultimate destination wedding that will occur sometime before the second coming of Jesus.

Destination weddings are hot! Brides today are seldom interested in getting married in the church in which they grew up. Destination weddings are the new, cool thing. Part of this is due to the outlandish preoccupation with the wedding event that often supersedes any concern for the marriage. It is also influenced by the fact that every generation wants to be different from the previous one.

Destination weddings usually take place in one of three types of settings:

1. An exotic, romantic spot at an incredibly expensive resort. A Caribbean beach is ideal. I performed a destination wedding a few years ago in the Caribbean where the whole wedding party was flown in and stayed at a five-star hotel on the father's tab. What a tab that must have been.

2. Another popular spot for destination weddings is in the great outdoors within an hour or two of where the bride lives—in a natural setting in the woods or a beautiful valley. This type of wedding causes the bride and her mother to double down in their prayer lives that it will not rain on the wedding day.

3. The third type of destination wedding often takes place in an urban setting in an older, rundown church facility that has a feeling of "authenticity." What an older, rundown church facility has to do with authenticity when the bride and groom never even think of attending that church is something I'm still trying to understand. But this choice causes me to chuckle. The church I pastor is in an ideal suburban setting and has a beautiful, traditional sanctuary. I remember when it was built I would hear young parents comment on what a beautiful place it would be for their daughter's wedding one day.

Yet today, most of their daughters wouldn't think of getting married in their home church—mainly because of its location in "the burbs." That would be more than the bride could bear.

Thankfully, the Bible has very exciting news about the ultimate destination wedding. The groom will be perfect, the bride will be spectacular, and the setting is literally out of this world. You won't want to miss it:

> Let us rejoice and be glad and give the glory to Him, for the marriage of the Lamb has come and His bride has made herself ready. (Rev. 19:7)

The groom is obviously Jesus. Jesus is referred to as the Lamb of God repeatedly in Scripture. When Jesus approached John the Baptist to be baptized, the stunned prophet exclaimed, "Behold, the Lamb of God who takes away the sin of the world" (John 1:29). "The Lamb" was the name He chose for Himself when He gave the apostle John this revelation.

On the occasion of His wedding feast, Jesus wants us to remember the price He paid for our sins. He is the sacrificial Lamb of God who has shed His blood to be our substitute—to take on the wrath of God's judgment for our sin. He is the true Lamb of God who has paid the ultimate price for His bride.

The Bride

Jesus's bride is the church. The church is not everyone who is a member of a Christian denomination. Countless lost people profess Jesus as Lord but have never really trusted

Christ as Savior and Lord. Jesus referred to these people in the Sermon on the Mount:

> Not everyone who says to Me, "Lord, Lord," will enter the kingdom of heaven, but he who does the will of My Father who is in heaven will enter. Many will say to Me on that day, "Lord, Lord, did we not prophesy in Your name, and in Your name cast out demons, and in Your name perform many miracles?" And then I will declare to them, "I never knew you; DEPART FROM ME, YOU WHO PRACTICE LAWLESS-NESS." (Matt. 7:21–23)

Many who profess Jesus as the Son of God are no different from the demons of hell (James 2:19). All through Jesus's ministry, the demons professed that Jesus is the Son of God (Matt. 8:29; Mark 1:34; Luke 4:41). They certainly are not Christians. They certainly won't be at this wedding feast.

No, the bride of Christ, the true church, are those who truly have been saved. They have been spiritually born as children of God. They have come to saving faith in Christ alone through His grace alone. These are the true followers of Jesus whom He has not only justified but also sanctified.

Ephesians 5:21–33 is probably the most important passage in the Bible regarding Christian marriage. It teaches that Christian marriage is to be a living testimony of the marriage of Christ, the groom, to His bride, the church. Christ chooses us and cleanses us to be His beautiful bride. His sanctification process begins with a cleansing of our souls at salvation. It continues all through our journey of faith to where He eventually makes us spiritually beautiful like a beautiful bride who has no spot or wrinkle and is holy and blameless. He does this through His love, His sacrifice, and the power of the Holy Spirit.

Our being prepared and ready is symbolized in Revelation 19:8:

> It was given to her to clothe herself in *fine linen, bright and clean*; for the fine linen is the righteous acts of the saints. (emphasis added)

Every bride wants to look beautiful in her wedding dress. The bright linen is symbolic of Christ clothing us in righteousness—holy and blameless.

Location of the Wedding

This wedding is the ultimate destination wedding because of its location at an out-of-this-world place called heaven. If this wedding feast occurs in heaven shortly before Jesus's second coming, then obviously the church will have been raptured at some point before He returns. But there is another reason to believe that.

In Revelation 19:14, Christ returns with his army:

> And the armies which are in heaven, *clothed in fine linen, white and clean*, were following Him on white horses. (emphasis added)

Scripture describes that army as wearing robes of fine linen exactly as it describes the bride's clothing in the wedding feast in Revelation 19:8. So the church will return with Christ when He comes again.

How students of Scripture come to conclude that the rapture of the church is not separate from the second coming of Christ is difficult to grasp. Yes, the timing of the rapture will surely be debated (and we'll look at that), but Revelation 19:7–9, 14 is convincing biblical evidence that the church will be raptured to heaven to be with Christ shortly before His second coming.

Who Will Be Invited?

> Then he said to me, "Write, 'Blessed are those who are invited to the marriage supper of the Lamb.'" And he said to me, "These are true words of God." (Rev. 19:9)

When a royal wedding occurs in Britain, whether it was Princess Diana and Prince Charles or Prince William and Kate, it's a big deal if you receive an invitation. Well, the wedding feast of the Lamb is the greatest of all wedding feasts. To receive an invitation is to be greatly blessed. So who will be invited?

It can't be the bride and groom, for they do the inviting. So if it is not Jesus and the church, who is it?

1. John the Baptist will be one: "He who has the bride is the bridegroom; but the friend of the bridegroom, who stands and hears him, rejoices greatly because of the bridegroom's voice. So this joy of mine has been made full" (John 3:29). He is clearly "the friend of the bridegroom."

2. Old Testament saints who were faithfully looking forward to the coming of the Messiah certainly seem to be good candidates for the invitation list.

3. Many believe it will include the angels as well.

One thing is for sure. It will be quite a celebration—an event we don't want to miss. If we are the bride—the church—we will be there. What a day it will be!

How will we get there? When will the church be taken up to heaven for this great celebration of the completed work of the church and the anticipation of the new life that is to come in Christ's second coming and the kingdom of God?

14

When the Trumpet Sounds

How We Get to the Ultimate Destination Wedding

Most people don't want to be left out of a big event, and the ultimate destination wedding will be the coolest of them all. Yet since it is literally "out of this world" (heaven), how do we get there? Do we have to die first? Well, that depends.

First of all, we have to be a follower of Jesus as our Savior and Lord. We have to be in the church—the bride of Christ. So if you are not a follower of Christ, there is no possible chance of being included in His wedding celebration.

Once we are Christ-followers, we will be included. Whether we have to die first depends on when Christ comes for His church. If He comes when we are alive, we get to escape death. If He does not come for His church before we die, then obviously our death precedes the big wedding celebration. That was the big concern of the Thessalonian Christians. That church was greatly concerned about Jesus's second coming. Many were worried that those who died before He came would be left out.

First Thessalonians 4:13 addresses the question:

> But we do not want you to be uninformed, brethren, about those who are asleep, so that you will not grieve as do the rest who have no hope.

Paul is reassuring. Our faith is unique because death is not the end. Yes, it is the great enemy of all men (1 Cor. 15:26). Nothing causes greater grief and heartache than death. Yet Christians grieve differently from the rest of the world. We grieve with hope. Because Jesus conquered death, so will we. Any separation from a Christian loved one who dies is a temporal separation. We will see them again. We live with a double hope—hope for eternal life with Jesus and hope that we'll see all those who have died in Christ again. As a pastor, I've been asked to conduct a few funerals for non-Christians. It is an inevitably sad and bleak feeling. It is an awful reality for loved ones left behind that they will never see their loved one again. This is why Christians grieve differently. Yes, there is great sadness at the separation that could be for a long time. Yet we live with the hope that we will one day be reunited with them in heaven.

Paul's word *asleep* means death and has caused some to wonder if when a Christian dies they are in a sleep-like state until Jesus comes again. No. Our physical bodies give out and die, but our souls—filled with the Spirit of the Lord— are instantly with the Lord in heaven. When the thief on the cross cried out to Jesus to remember him in paradise (a true sinner's prayer), Jesus said, "Today you shall be with Me in Paradise" (Luke 23:43).

This hope is strengthened with the promise that when Jesus comes for His church He will bring with Him those who have died in Christ.

> For if we believe that Jesus died and rose again, even so God will bring with Him those who have fallen asleep in Jesus. (1 Thess. 4:14)

Once again the expression *fallen asleep* is used in place of death. The origin of the word *cemetery* means "sleeping place."[1] Our bodies die and are buried and decay, yet our souls never die when they become inhabited by the Spirit of the Lord—the Holy Spirit—at the moment of salvation:

> For this we say to you by the word of the Lord, that we who are alive and remain until the coming of the Lord, will not precede those who have fallen asleep. (1 Thess. 4:15)

When Christ comes, those who have already died in Christ (whose souls are in heaven) obviously will be with the Lord first:

> For the Lord Himself will descend from heaven with a shout, with the voice of the archangel and with the trumpet of God, and the dead in Christ will rise first. (1 Thess. 4:16)

When the Lord comes for His people (the church) who are still alive here on this earth, there will be a great shout from heaven. I wonder if it will be like a massive sonic boom. This shout will come from the archangel.

Michael is named as the archangel in Daniel 12:1. Yet others believe there can be more than one with this title.

Some think it is possibly Gabriel. Whenever a really big announcement from heaven occurred, Gabriel was the man. He announced to Mary that God had chosen her to give birth to His son while she was still a virgin.

Whether it is Michael or Gabriel, we will know soon enough. It will be the shout heard around the world.

This will be followed by a sound of a trumpet. Trumpets (or shofars) in the Old Testament were used to call the children of Israel together. They were used for three occasions: 1) for a big announcement; 2) in a time of great celebration; or 3) a call to war. Jesus's second coming will include all of these. It announces the coming of Jesus for His church. It will announce the celebration of the wedding feast. And it will announce the call to war on the Antichrist and his followers. One thing is for sure—when the trumpet sounds, it will get everyone's attention. We will all take note.

Winston Churchill was a fascinating man. Many think he was the greatest man of the twentieth century. His funeral at St. Paul's Cathedral in London lived up to his reputation. Near the end, "Taps" was played. It is played in the military at the end of a day and appropriately at military funerals at the end of a life. Its haunting sound is always moving. Yet at Churchill's funeral after the end of "Taps," the trumpeter began to play "Reveille"—the wake-up call typically played at the beginning of a new day. At first people were confused, and some were appalled, and then a chuckle began to roll through the congregation as once again Churchill, even after his death, was making a statement they would never forget. He was reminding them that even though his life here on earth was over, as a Christian he would rise again to meet the Lord in heaven:

> Then we who are alive and remain will be caught up together
> with them in the clouds to meet the Lord in the air, and so
> we shall always be with the Lord. (1 Thess. 4:17)

The phrase *caught up together* is where we get the word
rapture. It literally means to "snatch up quickly." I realize
the word *rapture* never appears in the Bible, but neither does
the word *trinity*. Yet both doctrines are clearly taught in
Scripture.

It is during the events described in 1 Thessalonians 4:15–17
that followers of Christ are believed to receive a new resurrected body. Christ's resurrected body is "the first fruits of
those who are asleep" (1 Cor. 15:20). In other words, His
resurrected body is the picture of the type of body we will
receive when Christ comes for His church. Jesus's resurrected
body is different from the physical body He had here on the
earth. It is similar in that it is touchable. He told Thomas to
place his hands in the scars on His hands and His side (John
20:27). Jesus enjoyed good food with the disciples when He
held a fish fry with them on the shore of the Sea of Galilee
(John 21:10–13).

Yet Jesus's resurrected body is very different too. It is not
limited by time or space (he was able to appear and disap-
pear from a room; walls did not stop him). It is also a body
that never gets sick and diseased. This type of body will be
what Christians receive. It will be awesome. I'm sure looking forward to it.

First Corinthians 15:35–40 gives more insight:

> But someone will say, "How are the dead raised? And with
> what kind of body do they come?" You fool! That which
> you sow does not come to life unless it dies; and that which

you sow, you do not sow the body which is to be, but a bare grain, perhaps of wheat or of something else. But God gives it a body just as He wished, and to each of the seeds a body of its own. All flesh is not the same flesh, but there is one flesh of men, and another flesh of beasts, and another flesh of birds, and another of fish. There are also heavenly bodies and earthly bodies, but the glory of the heavenly is one, and the glory of the earthly is another.

Our resurrected bodies will be similar to our physical bodies yet different. Paul compared it to a seed and the plant that comes from it. The seed has to be buried in the ground before it springs to new life. Like a seed buried in the ground that comes up out of the earth as a plant or a tree, our physical bodies die and are buried (usually) and come up out of the earth new and different when Jesus comes for His church.

So what age will we look like? Twenty? Thirty? Fifty? Eighty? Oh, I hope not eighty or even fifty or twenty. I'd like about thirty. At twenty-two when I got married, I was so skinny. I don't know what my wife, Anne, saw in me—I was 6'1" and weighed all of 135 pounds. If I turned sideways, you couldn't see me. By thirty, her great home cooking had added some much-needed weight, and my focus on fitness had me in the best shape of my life. I think about thirty sounds good. Yet only God knows.

Whatever age we are, we will look better than we have ever looked on this earth. We will be dazzling like Jesus. Even better, our resurrected bodies will never have a single disability. They will never age and die. For all who trust in Jesus, this is mighty good news. We will all look our best for the wedding feast in heaven, and we will all look our best *forever*!

Thus, Paul closes this section of his letter with these words: "Therefore comfort one another with these words" (1 Thess. 4:18). For the Christian, whether we have died or are alive, it will be glorious. It will be a joy and celebration like we've never seen. This gives us great comfort.

One thing is for sure: you don't want to be left behind when the church is raptured.

15

No One Knows the Day or Hour

Four Rapture Theories

The rapture of the church is clearly taught in Scripture by show-ing that the wedding feast of Christ and His bride, the church, occurs sometime before Jesus's second coming. The rapture is also the way we get to the ultimate destination wedding in heaven. Now the question arises, When does the rapture occur?

First, remember this: to be dogmatic about when the rapture occurs is to go beyond Scripture. The Bible simply is not clear. We just know it will happen sometime before Jesus's second coming. There are four dominant views about the "when."

The No-Rapture Theory

Many fine, Bible-believing Christians believe this theory. Most of them argue that the doctrine of the rapture appeared in only the last 150 or so years of church history. Not only does this view ignore the biblical teaching of the wedding feast of Christ and His church occurring in heaven before His second coming, but it also ignores a key teaching of our Lord.

Jesus said this:

> Do not let your heart be troubled; believe in God, believe also in Me. In My Father's house are many dwelling places; if it were not so, I would have told you; for I go to prepare a place for you. If I go and prepare a place for you, I will come again and receive you to Myself, that where I am, there you may be also. And you know the way where I am going. (John 14:1–4)

Jesus was speaking of the many dwelling places He has prepared for His followers for when they die and go to heaven. Yet He very clearly said, "If I go and prepare a place for you, I will come back and take you to be with me, that you may be where I am." Jesus was referring to coming back for His church to join Him for the wedding feast. The second coming is not about joining Jesus forever *in* heaven. The second coming is Jesus returning *to* earth *from* heaven with His church.

Revelation 19:11–14 describes His glorious return. Verse 14 tells of the church returning with Him:

> And the armies which are in heaven, clothed in fine linen, white and clean, were following Him on white horses.

Those accompanying Christ—His army—will be clothed in fine linen! We've seen how this is the same description of the clothes worn by those in the church in Revelation 19:8 for the wedding feast: "It was given to her to clothe herself in fine linen, bright and clean; for the fine linen is the righteous acts of the saints." Looking at Scripture in light of Scripture clearly teaches the doctrine of the rapture of the church.

The Pre-Tribulation Rapture Theory

This is the most popular view held by evangelical Christians. The mega bestselling Left Behind series taught this view.

This theory teaches that the rapture will occur sometime before the seven-year tribulation period. Most probably, this will be before the Antichrist appears on the world scene and enters into a peace treaty with Israel.

Revelation 3:10 is often used as the proof text; it is part of Jesus's letter to the ancient church at Philadelphia:

> Because you have kept the word of My perseverance, *I also will keep you from the hour of testing*, that hour which is about to come upon the whole world, to test those who dwell on the earth. (emphasis added)

The argument is made that the church at Philadelphia is symbolic of the true church even though each of the seven churches of Revelation 2–3 were real, historical churches. Yes, they represent local churches in one way or another, but they were actual churches. The promise claimed in this view of the rapture is that all true Christians alive at the time of the rapture will be spared "that hour which is about to come upon the whole world."

My wife says she prefers this theory. If every Christian had their choice, I think we would all agree. Yet Jesus promised the opposite for His followers, all the way back to His original disciples. He promised that all of us would face tribulation. It is one way we identify with Jesus's suffering on the cross.

141

Yet the argument that is the most persuasive concerning the pre-tribulation rapture theory is the argument of "imminence." Jesus is clear that He will come like a thief in the night (Matt. 24:43; Rev. 16:15). He can come at any time. Thus, we are to be ready at all times: "Therefore be on the alert, for you do not know which day your Lord is coming" (Matt. 24:42). The pre-tribulation rapture theory best meets this teaching.

The Post-Tribulation Rapture Theory

According to this view, the church will go through the entire tribulation period described in Revelation 6–18. The church will not be spared of anything—even the Great Tribulation period after the Abomination of Desolation at which time the Antichrist declares himself God in the temple and all hell breaks loose on the face of the earth.

The best argument for this view is where the wedding feast falls in Revelation 19:7–10. It is right before Jesus's second coming described in Revelation 19:11–19. So if Revelation 19 is written in chronological order, this view makes the most sense.

The Mid-Tribulation Rapture Theory

This is the view that makes the most sense to me. Why? First, Jesus promised that His church would face tribulation. No doubt, the church has faced tribulation in every age all the way back to the first disciples. Why should it be any different at the end of the age?

Second, Paul writes that the apostasy of the church must occur first. This has already happened in Europe and with much of the American church today.

Third, Paul writes that the Antichrist will appear on the world scene and halfway through the seven-year peace treaty with Israel will put a stop to sacrifices at the rebuilt temple. This will follow soon after he has entered the temple and declared himself God in an effort to unite the world around worshiping him. Israel will rebel against this abomination. Paul writes that this will occur only when the restrainer, the Holy Spirit through the church, is removed from the world's scene (2 Thess. 2:6–7). Obviously, Christians in the church will have been raptured by that time.

Can we be sure of this timing? Absolutely not. Scripture provides hints but is not clear on the timing. Yet one thing Jesus did make clear is that the preaching of the gospel of the kingdom to every people group on the face of the earth must be done before the end will come (Matt. 24:14). Since almost 3,100 of the over 11,000 people groups in the world still have not been engaged with the gospel, our calling is urgent as history races toward the end of the age.

I do believe two examples of Jesus's teaching about His second coming add to the understanding of the rapture of the church.

1. Matthew 24:37–41

> For the coming of the Son of Man will be just like the days of Noah. For as in those days before the flood they were eating and drinking, marrying and giving in marriage, until the day that Noah entered the ark, and they did not understand until the flood came and took them all away; so will the coming of the Son of Man be. Then there will be two men in the field; one will be taken and

143

one will be left. Two women will be grinding at the mill; one will be taken and one will be left.

Noah and the ark were lifted up to escape God's judgment in the flood. Those who faced judgment were left behind. They were not taken up in the ark with Noah to escape judgment.

Yet when God's judgment in the world was complete, the ark was slowly lowered back down to the earth when the floodwaters receded. Do you see the picture of the rapture? The church is raised to the wedding feast in heaven with Jesus while God brings judgment on the earth during the Great Tribulation. Then when Christ's judgment is being completed at Jesus's second coming, the church is lowered back down to the earth to reign with Him.

2. **Matthew 25:1–13.** Jesus told the parable of the ten virgins, who were the equivalent of bridesmaids for a wedding:

> Then the kingdom of heaven will be comparable to ten virgins, who took their lamps and went out to meet the bridegroom. Five of them were foolish, and five were prudent. For when the foolish took their lamps, they took no oil with them, but the prudent took oil in flasks along with their lamps. Now while the bridegroom was delaying, they all got drowsy and began to sleep. But at midnight there was a shout, "Behold, the bridegroom! Come out to meet him." Then all those virgins rose and trimmed their lamps. The foolish said to the prudent, "Give us some of your oil, for our lamps are going out." But the prudent answered, "No, there will not be enough for us and you too; go instead to the dealers and buy some for yourselves." And while they

144

were going away to make the purchase, the bridegroom came, and those who were ready went in with him to the wedding feast; and the door was shut. Later the other virgins also came, saying, "Lord, lord, open up for us." But he answered, "Truly I say to you, I do not know you." Be on the alert then, for you do not know the day nor the hour.

In this parable, the groom comes for his bride. When he does, five virgins are ready and five are not. First-century Jewish weddings would begin when the groom left his father's house to go to the bride's house and bring her back to his father's house for the wedding. When the groom arrived at the bride's home, he would then lead her through the streets of the village with her bridesmaids. The whole village would come out to celebrate with the groom and the bride as they returned to his father's house. In Jesus's parable, five bridesmaids were ready and five were not.

What a beautiful and sobering picture of the rapture as Jesus leaves his father in heaven to retrieve his bride, the church. Some will be ready, and some will not.

None of us knows for sure when the rapture will occur, yet Scripture makes clear that it will occur. We want to be ready when He comes, and we want to be watchful in anticipation of His coming. Being ready means being sure of salvation and eternal life in Christ. If you are the least bit unsure of your salvation, you want to be sure. If somebody asks you, "If Christ came today, would you be ready?" you don't have to respond, "I hope so" or "I want to be." In Christ, we can say, "Absolutely, but not because I deserve to be. I don't deserve

to be at all. But in Christ I have the promise of eternal life."
(See 1 John 5:12.)

Then, when we are ready in Christ, we want to live watchfully, knowing that Jesus can come for His church at any time. At the same time, Scripture is so clear about events that will happen before He comes that we need not be surprised that the rapture is near when these biblical events prophesied begin to unfold.

One thing is for sure, when Jesus comes for His church, we want to be living in a way that is pleasing to Him. That means being focused on the mission He has given us—to follow Him as a fisher of people for those with whom our lives intersect and to support ministry that seeks to take the good news to every people group on this earth.

16

Armageddon

A Great Battle in the Valley of Slaughter

When Christians have left the scene and the church is no longer around to be salt and light in a dead and dark world, the stage will be set for Armageddon. Most people are aware of this term. Even secularists and people of other religions tend to know that it is the final climactic battle between good and evil.

Apocalyptic imagery is associated with Armageddon. Hollywood has developed a whole genre of movies that are nothing more than glorified action video games. In these movies, courageous underdogs battle monstrous, "beastlike" evil forces that are hell-bent on destroying the earth and all humankind. Doomsday scenarios abound.

Yet the Bible, not Hollywood, gives us the truth about Armageddon. God's Word reveals how events will unfold to lead to that climactic moment in history. So what does it say?

And I saw coming out of the mouth of the dragon and out of the mouth of the beast and out of the mouth of the false prophet, three unclean spirits like frogs; for they are spirits of demons, performing signs, which go out to the kings of the whole world, to gather them together for the war of the great day of God, the Almighty. ("Behold, I am coming like a thief. Blessed is the one who stays awake and keeps his clothes, so that he will not walk about naked and men will not see his shame.") And they gathered them together to the place which in Hebrew is called Har-Magedon. (Rev. 16:13–16)

Most of the time spiritual warfare is invisible. The Bible tells us "our struggle is not against flesh and blood, but against the rulers, against the powers, against the world forces of this darkness, against the spiritual forces of wickedness in the heavenly places" (Eph. 6:12). Spiritual forces are associated with the invisible, for the spiritual can't be seen. Yet these invisible forces are very real and very powerful. Any Christian who seeks to fulfill God's will by sharing and advancing the kingdom will begin to experience spiritual warfare. The devil will use distractions and conflict in the body to take our focus off our mission. He will use out-and-out opposition that will seem to be simply evil human opposition to a Christ-centered morality. Christians on the frontlines of ministry soon realize that the enemy is doing anything he can to prevent the advancement of the gospel.

Yet in the final days of Armageddon, when the church is gone and the Antichrist is consolidating his one-world government at an extraordinary pace, spiritual warfare will then be visible. It will be seen in the demonic trinity that we looked at in chapter 11. Remember, the devil is the great counterfeiter. He wants to replace God with himself. The

Bible is clear that there is only one God in three persons. He is Father, Son, and Holy Spirit.

As human beings, our finite minds are never able to completely grasp God as three persons in one. I've tried to explain it by using the example that I am known three ways in my family. I am the father to my three sons, and they know me one way. I'm the son of my parents, and they have known me in another way. I'm the husband to my wife, and she knows me another way. Yet in all three roles, I'm the same person. Yet this is a wholly inadequate analogy of the Trinity, for how do we explain God the Son praying to God the Father? It boggles our minds. We can never completely grasp it. That in and of itself is a reminder of how great God is and how small we are.

However, the devil wants to counterfeit this greatness, and we see that in the demonic trinity.

The dragon is the devil; the beast is the Antichrist, the incarnation of the devil; and the false prophet plays a counterfeit role of the Holy Spirit. They will work together to try to force the whole world to worship and submit to the Antichrist.

Through the Antichrist and the false prophet, spiritual warfare will be visible. Armageddon will be a day when the demonic trinity will be clearly seen from heaven by Christ and His raptured church. Yet even though it will be visible, the world will be blinded to the "spiritual warfare" of what is about to occur. It will appear that the Antichrist is an all-powerful, unstoppable force for world unity. King after king and nation after nation will be in awe of his supernatural power. The world will worship and follow him. They simply will not see what is happening.

Even the nations of the East—of Asia—will be enamored with his greatness, and the sovereign God of the universe will have prepared the way for armies of the East to join the mighty army of nations from all over the world. How will they get to Armageddon in Israel? Some will come by air for sure. But the millions of ground troops will now have had a great barrier removed—by now the great Euphrates River has dried up:

> The sixth angel poured out his bowl on the great river, the Euphrates; and its water was dried up, so that the way would be prepared for the kings from the east. (Rev. 16:12)

The Euphrates is one of the great rivers of the world. It is more than one thousand miles long and begins at the base of Mount Ararat in modern-day Turkey and runs all the way to the Persian Gulf. If ground troops tried to travel by foot to Armageddon today, the Euphrates River would halt their path.

It is at its grandest in modern-day Iraq, northeast of Israel. To think of the Euphrates drying up is as astounding as imagining the mighty Mississippi River drying up. Yet God will do all this to prepare the way for the kings of the East to join forces with the Antichrist in preparation for Jesus's return.

They will come together for war on the "Great Day of the Lord," which is a term used over and over in Scripture to describe a great day of God's judgment on all the earth at the end of the age. This is important. God is in charge of these unfolding events. It will appear to the world that one man is in charge—the Antichrist. He will be at the height of his power. The world will be in awe of his supernatural power and greatness. Yet God will be orchestrating the events. I love what the second psalm prophesies about Armageddon:

> The kings of the earth take their stand and the rulers take counsel together against the LORD and against His Anointed, saying, "Let us tear their fetters apart and cast away their cords from us!" He who sits in the heavens laughs, the Lord scoffs at them. (Ps. 2:2–4)

The devil will be gloating. The Antichrist will feel invincible. The false prophet will be cheering him on. But God will be laughing in heaven with a mocking laughter at the arrogance of the demonic trinity that is about to face the judgment of God.

But there is one hugely important question: Who is the Antichrist coming to fight? Scripture tells us it is God in Christ. Yet can you imagine the nations of the world being gathered with great military might under the Antichrist to battle Jesus? The Antichrist will have charisma and leadership like no other world leader in history, yet no world leader would be taken seriously in leading world armies against Jesus, who lived two thousand years ago. They would see him as a crackpot—a nut. Besides, the Antichrist will not believe in Jesus. He will have already declared himself God when he entered the rebuilt temple in Jerusalem. He's not going to lead troops to do battle against someone he believes is long dead.

Some say that he will be gathering the troops to battle the church. Yet the church will have been raptured. Christians will be in heaven, and the church members left behind (cultural Christians) will be followers of the Antichrist. He will have co-opted the institutional church filled with cultural Christians into his show of worldwide support for unity and peace.

So who will he and his troops fight? The location reveals the answer:

> And they gathered them together to the place which in Hebrew is called Har-Magedon. (Rev. 16:16)

This is where we get the term Armageddon. *Har* means "mountain." *Magedon* stands for Megiddo, which means "place of slaughter."

Mount Megiddo is located in modern-day Israel and is appropriately named, for it is a unique place. About twenty-five civilizations have been built over one another. Archaeologists vary in regard to the exact number. Either way, it's a bunch. The layers began to be uncovered in 1903, and archaeologists continue to dig.[1] Archaeologically and geographically, this is one of the world's most important sites.

Why did this happen—one civilization conquering another and rebuilding on Mount Megiddo—atop what many of us would describe as a big hill?

Photo credit: Todd Bolen/BiblePlaces.com.

Tel Megiddo.

Mount Megiddo looks over the Valley of Jezreel, which is seen as the valley of Armageddon, the place where the Antichrist will gather troops from the nations of the world. This mountain is important historically because whoever controlled this spot controlled the ancient trade route that connected three continents—Africa, Asia, and Europe. When Napoleon stood on Mount Megiddo and looked over the valley, he said, "All the armies of the world could maneuver their forces on this vast plain."[2]

When my wife and I lead Bible study tours of Israel, it is one of my favorite places to visit. When you stand on Mount Megiddo and look out over the Valley of Jezreel, it is easy to visualize millions of troops gathered there. It is one awesome site. I envision troops that have come from the east along the Jordan River and troops that have arrived from the southwest from the Mediterranean Sea.

Photo credit: Austin Smith.

Jezreel Valley.

Yet why the battle? Why will they gather to fight? Once again, the location gives us the answer: *Israel*.

Remember that when the Antichrist enters the rebuilt temple in Jerusalem and declares himself God, Israel will rebel. Even though most of the Jews in modern-day Israel are secular or nonreligious, they have a heritage as a monotheistic people. They will rebel against the idea of a man declaring himself God.

The Antichrist will then respond like all megalomaniacs who want to be all-powerful and center everyone's focus on themselves. He will be furious. In his outrage, he will order a stop to sacrifices at the temple (Dan. 9:27), and he will call together the nations of the world to destroy this little troublemaker nation of Jews once and for all. Being the shrewd politician he will be, he will justify this as the last resort and hope for peace in the Middle East.

God loves the Jews. He has a special place for the Jews. Thus, the devil hates the Jews. All through history the Antichrist-type characters have sought to destroy the Jews or blame the Jews or expel the Jews from their land. From Nebuchadnezzar of Babylon, who leveled Jerusalem; to Haman, the prime minister of Persia as described in the book of Esther; to the Roman Emperor Claudius, who ordered all the Jews expelled from Rome; to Adolf Hitler, who murdered approximately six million Jews in the Holocaust; to modern-day Islamists in Iran and all over the Middle East—anti-Semitism is the devil's major fuel.

What is astounding is the rise of anti-Semitism in Europe today—Europe, the land of the Holocaust. How can it be? Look at these headlines from 2014 and 2015:

"Exodus: Why Europe's Jews are Fleeing Once Again"[3]

"Anti-Semitism on Rise across Europe 'in Worst Times Since the Nazis'"[4]

"Europe's Anti-Semitism Comes Out of the Shadows"[5]

"The Return of Anti-Semitism"[6]

"Anti-Semitic Violence Surged 40% Worldwide Last Year"[7]

"Is It Time for the Jews to Leave Europe?"[8]

There is even growing anti-Semitism among some of the academic elite in American universities. Just note these headlines:

"Majoring in Anti-Semitism at Vassar"[9]

"Ohio Professor Keeps Job Despite Spewing Anti-Semitic Hate on Social Media"[10]

"Anti-Semitic Incidents on US College Campuses Spike"[11]

Yet what makes this anti-Semitism so insidious is that it is couched as opposition to the State of Israel, not the Jews themselves. This is pure nonsense.

Manuel Valls, Socialist prime minister of France, said:

> It is legitimate to criticize the policies of Israel. This criticism exists in Israel itself. But this is not what we are talking about in France. This is radical criticism of the very existence of Israel, which is anti-Semitic. There is an incontestable link between anti-Zionism and anti-Semitism. Behind anti-Zionism is anti-Semitism.
>
> Frequently, anti-Zionists let the mask slip. It is impossible to ascribe the attacks on synagogues—at least eight were targeted in France last summer—to anger over Israel's Gaza policy. The demonstrators who chanted 'Hamas, Hamas, Jews to the gas' at rallies in Germany last year clearly have more on their minds than Israel's West Bank settlement policy.[12]

When Prime Minister Netanyahu spoke to the US Congress on March 3, 2015, he sounded the alarm about the danger of the United States negotiating a bad deal with Iran on nuclear arms. Sadly, his clarion call fell on the deaf ears of President Obama, who symbolizes the growing lack of support for Israel among the academic and political elite even in America—the one nation that historically has been Israel's greatest ally.

Later in October 2015, Mr. Netanyahu addressed the United Nations. He said:

> The UN should finally rid itself of the obsessive bashing of Israel. Here's just one absurd example of this obsession: In four years of horrific violence in Syria, more than a quarter of a million people have lost their lives. That is more than

10 times the number of Israelis and Palestinians combined who have lost their lives in a century of conflict between us. Yet last year, this assembly adopted 20 resolutions against Israel and just one resolution about the savage slaughter in Syria. Talk about injustice. Talk about disproportionality. Twenty. Count them. Once against Syria.[13]

In an opinion piece for the *New York Times* in March 2015, Ron Prosor writes:

In 2013, Iran was elected to the committee responsible for disarmament—even as it continued its nuclear expansion, support for terrorism and the destruction of Israel. . . . Knowing this history, perhaps we shouldn't be surprised that, in the 2014–15 session alone, the General Assembly adopted about 20 resolutions critical of Israel, while the human rights situations in Iran, Syria, and North Korea merited just one condemnation apiece. . . . Nowhere is anti-Israel bias more obvious than in the Geneva-based Human Rights Council. . . . Israel is the only nation that is singled out for criticism by virtue of a special program, known as Agenda Item 7. A result, according to the Geneva-based monitoring group UN Watch, is that more than 50 percent of all condemnatory resolutions are directed at the Jewish state.[14]

Sadly, by the time of Armageddon, the United States' support and defense of Israel will have dissipated. The biblical basis for supporting Israel no longer will be a factor in the United States, for the Christians will have left the scene. By then anti-Semitism, that is straight from the pits of hell, will have swept the world like an unstoppable force. The Antichrist and the false prophet will be leading the charge. They will blame Israel and the Jews for conflict in the Middle

East, and they will be furious that Israel had the audacity to rebel against the Antichrist as god after all he had done for them in signing the peace treaty with them prophesied in Daniel 9:27. They will argue, "Eliminate Israel, and we'll have peace in the Middle East. With peace in the Middle East, there will be peace in all the world." All the people of the world will hypnotically buy into these demonic words like the Germans did with Hitler and his rampant anti-Semitism. Things will look bleak for Israel. It will be surrounded with nowhere to turn.

The situation will look hopeless, yet God will have the final say! The Old Testament prophet Zechariah wrote of specific details concerning Armageddon. His words are a sobering warning and a tremendous hope for the future of Israel. Back to the Old Testament we go for God's Word to give us the full picture of His future plans.

17

An Unbelievable Spectacle Witnessed by the World

A Jewish Prophet Explains Armageddon

Did you know that the events around Armageddon are more than a great battle? Did you know that a future attack on Jerusalem and Israel may take the lives of more Jews than the Holocaust? Did you know that prophesied events leading up to Armageddon are happening right before our eyes in Israel at this very hour?

An unheralded Old Testament Jewish prophet fills in the details of the events around Armageddon. When his prophecy and the teaching of the New Testament are combined, we get the full picture. That prophet's name is Zechariah. He revealed to the Jews details of events leading up to the coming of the Messiah.

The Battle of Jerusalem

> Behold, a day is coming for the LORD when the spoil taken from you will be divided among you. For I will gather all the nations against Jerusalem to battle, and the city will be captured, the houses plundered, the women ravished and half of the city exiled, but the rest of the people will not be cut off from the city. (Zech. 14:1–2)

The Antichrist's troops will storm into Jerusalem like the SS Nazis stormed into the Jewish ghettos of Poland during World War II. It will be a terrifying time for the Jews of Israel:

> "It will come about in all the land," declares the LORD, "That two parts in it will be cut off and perish; but the third will be left in it." (Zech. 13:8)

Two-thirds of the Jews will be killed, and only one-third will survive. This is a terrifying prophecy.

The world has already experienced one Holocaust during which 6 million Jews were exterminated by Hitler's Nazi Germany. In 1939, there were 16.6 million Jews in the world. Of those, 9.5 million lived in Europe. That was 57 percent of the Jews in the world. By 1945, the Jewish population of Europe had shrunk to about 3.8 million or 35 percent of the 11 million Jews in the world after World War II.[1]

Today there are about 16 million Jews in the world—around .002 percent of the world's population. This miniscule number is amazing when you consider their extraordinary influence on the approximately 7.5 billion people in the world.[2] Their achievements in the face of untold opposition, persecution, and hardship are amazing.

160

Of those approximately 16 million Jews, 6.1 million live in Israel (38 percent of the Jews in the world) and 5.7 million live in the United States.[3] Yet with the world's growing anti-Semitism, the number of Jews immigrating to Israel in coming years will be significant. What is happening in Europe has already happened in the Muslim countries of the Middle East. With the rebirth of Israel in 1948, the ingathering of Jews back to Israel has skyrocketed.

On a recent mission trip to minister to Syrian refugees who have fled to Lebanon, I asked our host how many Lebanese Jewish families were left in Lebanon. He replied, "I think five or six." Incredible! This too is a direct fulfillment of biblical prophecy, especially from Isaiah, Jeremiah, and Ezekiel. When I first went to Israel in the early 1990s, it was a time of massive immigration of Russian Jews due to the fall of communism. I was stunned to see all of the Old Testament prophecy of the ingathering of the Jews unfolding right before my eyes. Take a moment to read some of these prophecies of "the ingathering" to discover biblical prophecy that is happening today. It is amazing.

- Psalm 106:47
- Isaiah 11:12–13
- Jeremiah 23:2–6; 29:14; 30:2–9; 31:8, 10–12
- Ezekiel 11:16–20; 28:25–26; 34:13; 36:8–12, 21–38; 37:21–23, 25–28; 39:25–29

Wait! Don't skip over all these passages. It will astound you that all these prophetic passages are being (or have been) fulfilled. This will not stop. In the days ahead, the number of Jews in the diaspora will only decrease, and the number of Jews in Israel will increase.

What this means, in light of Zechariah's prophecy that two-thirds of the Jews will be killed in the battles in and around Jerusalem, is that the numbers could be greater than the Holocaust.

Why would God allow something so horrific to happen? God's sovereignty is often difficult to grasp. Yet all throughout biblical history, God has used pagan rulers to bring judgment on the Jewish people when they have turned away from God or grown hard-hearted toward Him. He did it through Nebuchadnezzar of Babylon in the destruction of Jerusalem and the Babylonian captivity of many Jews. Even though God warned them through the prophet Jeremiah, they refused to repent. In AD 70, in fulfillment of Jesus's prophecy in Matthew 24:1–2, Rome leveled the temple in Jerusalem and began the process of dispersing Jews away from their Promised Land of Israel to the four corners of the earth. This was God's judgment on Israel because of their hard-heartedness in rejecting His Son, the Messiah Jesus, one of their own kinsmen.

Today, the majority of Jews in Israel are not religious—they are Zionists. If there is a national idolatry in Israel today, it is Zionism. The second of the Ten Commandments is very clear: God is a jealous God who condemns us for putting any idol before him. Many secular Jews do this in Zionism.

Israel is also home to Orthodox (or religious) Jews, who make up about 15 percent of the Jews in Israel.[4] Like the nonreligious Jews, they have rejected Jesus as the Messiah. Unlike secular Jews, the Orthodox Jews do so because they feel that Jesus did not qualify as the Messiah from Old Testament prophecy. Though there are exciting movements in

Israel of Jews accepting Jesus as their Messiah, these overall numbers are still very small.

Zechariah 13:8 speaks to a future time of God's judgment on the Jewish people. Yet, God's judgment will not be the end of Israel, nor will it ever be. The remaining one-third of the Jews of Israel who survive will come through the fires of suffering.

They will be refined in their faith when they will call on God for help. How does this happen?

Remember, by now the main ally of Israel, the United States, has long since withdrawn its support. So with the United States no longer a staunch ally and protector of Israel, American troops will probably be gathered with other troops of the Antichrist at Armageddon. This will add to the terror of Jewish Israelis. They will feel doomed and all alone in the world. Yet they will have a secret weapon that they have foolishly forgotten—God has not forsaken them:

> In that day the LORD will defend the inhabitants of Jerusalem, and the one who is feeble among them in that day will be like David, and the house of David will be like God, like the angel of the LORD before them. And in that day I will set about to destroy all the nations that come against Jerusalem. (Zech. 12:8–9)

God will destroy those troops of many nations under the Antichrist. How will this happen?

When the troops are gathered at Armageddon, the Jews of Israel will realize they have nowhere to turn but God to save them from extermination. They will do what many non-believers do in a life-and-death situation. They will cry out to God. We can picture their prayer: "Oh God, save us! Send us the Messiah! It is our only hope." God will answer their prayers. The Messiah will appear in the clouds, and to their shock and amazement, it will be Jesus.

He will appear in the sky for all the world to see.

Jesus described what his return will be like:

> And then the sign of the Son of Man will appear in the sky, and then all the tribes of the earth will mourn, and they will see the SON of MAN COMING ON THE CLOUDS OF THE SKY with power and great glory. (Matt. 24:30)

Oh, come on. The earth is round. Jesus will appear in the clouds over Jerusalem. The view in the Americas will be totally blocked by the earth. Yet everyone will see because at Armageddon the world's press will be out in force. The press loves a spectacle—a show of military might. They will have their cameras pointed at the Antichrist's army. Then, when all eyes turn toward the clouds, their cameras will too. The world will see it on every major news network—not to mention the internet or smartphones or many other tools of media. This will be a day of great mourning for every tribe and nation on earth. For this will be the Great Day of the Lord. People will finally see Jesus for who He is in all of His glory and holiness. Conviction of sin will result for everyone who has rejected Christ.

Yet when the Jews see it is Jesus, they will mourn differently. Yes, there will be great conviction of sin knowing that they and most of their forefathers have rejected God's Son as Messiah for almost two thousand years. But their mourning will be overpowered by God's grace as they cry out for God's mercy while knowing they deserve God's judgment. Amazingly, God will show them His awesome grace:

I will pour out on the house of David and on the inhabitants of Jerusalem, the Spirit of grace and of supplication, so that they will look on Me whom they have pierced; and they will mourn for Him, as one mourns for an only son, and they will weep bitterly over Him like the bitter weeping over a firstborn. (Zech. 12:10)

Jesus was speaking through the prophet in the words, "They will look on Me whom they have pierced." The "Me" is capitalized to indicate divinity. The "piercing" is a clear reference to the cross. Jesus went on to refer to how they will "mourn" with conviction of their sins for rejecting God's "only son" for so long. This will lead to the "bitter weeping" that occurs when sinners finally see Jesus and are convicted of their sins. This mourning for sin is essential to anyone who comes to salvation through faith in Jesus's grace. Yet here it will be both individual and corporate mourning of a whole people group that has been so blessed and yet so hardened against God's Son.

Look where this occurs:

In that day there will be great mourning in Jerusalem, like the mourning of Hadadrimmon in the plain of Megiddo. (Zech. 12:11)

The Jews of Israel mourning over their sin and crying out for the grace of God will lead to a huge momentum change at Armageddon. It will shift from the Antichrist, an unstoppable force in destroying Israel, to Jesus, the Messiah and Savior, coming to save Israel from extermination. But even more, He will come to save them from their sins. God has not given up on His specially chosen people. He never has. He never will. He has great plans for Israel. In that Great

Day of the Lord, all the world will see it. It will be God's ultimate show of grace.

Just as Christ's first coming was the turning point in all of history, His second coming will be the turning point in all of history for the Jews that He has come to save. It is one of the two big reasons Armageddon will be the climactic event in all of history.

Back to the new covenant. The Jewish prophet Zechariah has filled in many of the details as his words speak to Jews and Christians alike. We will return to his prophecy. Yet it is the new covenant and the writings of the apostle Paul that reveal to us what will happen when the Jews at Armageddon come to repentant faith in Jesus as their Messiah.

18

God's Irrevocable Promise

The Salvation of Israel
and the Hope of Gentiles

Some of the most common questions I am asked have to do with the Jews.

"What about the Jews? If they are God's chosen people, why do the majority reject Jesus as the Messiah?"

"Will the Jews go to heaven or hell?"

"Will the Jews be saved?"

In Romans 9, 10, and 11, the apostle Paul shares his heart for his fellow Jews. He also answers those questions. In Romans 9:1–5, he writes that he wants God's chosen people to come to faith in Christ:

> I am telling the truth in Christ, I am not lying, my conscience testifies with me in the Holy Spirit, that I have great sorrow

and unceasing grief in my heart. For I could wish that I myself were accursed, separated from Christ for the sake of my brethren, my kinsmen according to the flesh, who are Israelites, to whom belongs the adoption as sons, and the glory and the covenants and the giving of the Law and the temple service and the promises, whose are the fathers, and from whom is the Christ according to the flesh, who is over all, God blessed forever. Amen.

Paul was obviously burdened for his kinsmen to come to repentant faith in Christ—so much so that he was willing to be "cursed" (sentenced to hell) if some of them would. That is extraordinary, selfless love for his people.

Then in Romans 11:1–2, Paul makes it clear that God had not rejected His people:

I say then, God has not rejected His people, has He? May it never be! For I too am an Israelite, a descendant of Abraham, of the tribe of Benjamin. God has not rejected His people whom He foreknew. Or do you not know what the Scripture says in the passage about Elijah, how he pleads with God against Israel?

Then in Romans 11:25, he summarizes what he had been trying to explain—why so many Jews have remained hardened against the gospel of Christ:

For I do not want you, brethren, to be uninformed of this mystery—so that you will not be wise in your own estimation—that a partial hardening has happened to Israel until the fullness of the Gentiles has come in.

In Romans 11, Paul lets us know we should not be surprised that most Jews are resistant to the gospel. A remnant of Jews has believed Jesus was the Messiah ever since His ministry here on earth, but most Jews have had their hearts hardened against Jesus as their Messiah for almost two thousand years.

Yet God in His mercy and love for the Gentiles has allowed us to be grafted into the tree of faith:

> I say then, they [Jews] did not stumble so as to fall, did they [Jews]? May it never be! But by their transgression salvation has come to the Gentiles, to make them jealous. Now if their transgression is riches for the world and their failure is riches for the Gentiles, how much more will their fulfillment be! . . . But if some of the branches were broken off, and you, being a wild olive, were grafted in among them and became partaker with them of the rich root of the olive tree, do not be arrogant toward the branches; but if you are arrogant, remember that it is not you who supports the root, but the root supports you. . . . And they [Jews] also, if they [Jews] do not continue in their unbelief, will be grafted in, for God is able to graft them in again. For if you were cut off from what is by nature a wild olive tree, and were grafted contrary to nature into a cultivated olive tree, how much more will these who are the natural branches be grafted into their own olive tree? (Rom. 11:11–12, 17–18, 23–24)

The Jews are the roots, but we Gentile Christians are the branches. We have not replaced the Jews as God's chosen people, but we have been grafted in by God's grace because of a partial hardening of the Jews against Jesus. Replacement theology—that the church has "replaced" Israel in God's covenant—is simply not biblical. Yet some Christians believe and teach this. They are wrong! This time in history is the age when the Gentile-led church has a mission to take the gospel of Christ's kingdom to every people group on the face of the earth. When that mission is complete, the church will be raptured into heaven for the ultimate destination wedding to celebrate the completion of the mission and look with anticipation to returning to earth with Jesus at His second coming and reigning with Him.

Through the years, though, God has not forgotten the Jews whom He has chosen and loves so much. His grace will be lavishly poured out on them when Israel is surrounded and seemingly doomed in the day of Armageddon. When they cry to God to send the Messiah to save them from extermination, He will not only do so, but through His grace, He will also lead the Jews of Israel to nationwide repentance and faith. This leads to very good news:

> And so all Israel will be saved; just as it is written, "THE DELIVERER WILL COME FROM ZION, HE WILL REMOVE UNGODLINESS FROM JACOB. THIS IS MY COVENANT WITH THEM, WHEN I TAKE AWAY THEIR SINS." (Rom. 11:26–27)

All Israel will be saved. They will be saved when their deliverer, Jesus the Messiah from Zion (Jerusalem), comes to bring judgment on the Antichrist and his followers. It will be the climactic moment in all of history.

It will be doubly good news for Israel. The Jews will not only be saved physically from extinction, but they will also be saved spiritually: "HE WILL REMOVE UNGODLINESS FROM JACOB" (Rom. 11:26). Jacob was the grandson of Abraham. He was a lying, scheming mama's boy until he had an all-night wrestling match with God—his dark night of the soul.

God then changed Jacob's name to Israel, from which the nation of Israel comes. Jacob represents sinful man—before his life is transformed by God's grace and power. The Deliverer, Jesus the Messiah, comes at this climactic moment of history to save the Jews, Jacob (now Israel), from their sin.

God's new covenant with these redeemed Jews at the end of the age will be the fulfillment of Jeremiah's prophecy:

"Behold, days are coming," declares the LORD, "when I will make a new covenant with the house of Israel and with the house of Judah, not like the covenant which I made with their fathers in the day I took them by the hand to bring them out of the land of Egypt, My covenant which they broke, although I was a husband to them," declares the LORD. "But this is the covenant which I will make with the house of Israel after those days," declares the LORD, "I will put My law within them and on their heart I will write it; and I will be their God, and they shall be My people. They will not teach again, each man his neighbor and each man his brother, saying, 'Know the LORD,' for they will all know Me, from the least of them to the greatest of them," declares the LORD, "for I will forgive their iniquity, and their sin I will remember no more." (Jer. 31:31–34)

God will take away their sin. They will be filled with His Holy Spirit. The law of God and their desire to please Him will be written on their hearts, and they will live in a way that is pleasing to Him.

At last, all that God had hoped for when He chose Abraham, Isaac, and Jacob will be realized. It will be glorious. There will be rejoicing among all God's children—Jews and Gentiles—as never before.

Then God's Word explains why we Gentile Christians, while knowing the Jews are God's chosen people, have dealt with such frustration regarding the their hard-hearted resistance to Jesus as the Messiah:

> From the standpoint of the gospel they are enemies for your sake, but from the standpoint of God's choice they are beloved for the sake of the fathers; for the gifts and the calling of God are irrevocable. (Rom. 11:28–29)

Right now, most Jews are enemies of the gospel for the sake of Gentiles. God has grafted Gentile believers into the family of faith in this time in history when most Jews have an almost irrational hostility to the gospel and the name of Jesus. Gentiles are certainly not "grafted in" because we deserve to be. None of us do. It is so only by God's grace.

Yet God has not rejected the Jews. They are beloved because of God's calling and promises to Abraham, Isaac, and Jacob: "For the gifts and the calling are irrevocable." Irrevocable means unchanging. Irrevocable means they have not been reversed. Irrevocable means permanent. The calling cannot be broken.

Throughout history the world has seen the incredible giftedness of the Jewish people; they have been awarded more Nobel Prizes than any other people group. And no minority has ever been persecuted and discriminated against like the Jews, yet time and time again they rise above it all.

When the number of Jews began to grow and excel dramatically in America's best universities, some in higher education pushed for quotas to limit the number of Jewish students (much like some try to do with Asian students today).[1] By 1919, Jews made up 40 percent of Columbia University.

And in 1922, they comprised 21 percent of the freshman class at Harvard, after being only 7 percent in 1900. So that year Harvard's president proposed limiting the number of Jewish students.[2]

Despite all the discrimination, bigotry, hatred, and resentment, Jewish people have continued to prove that they are amazingly gifted, bright, and industrious. And even though many Jewish people do not believe in Jesus as the Messiah, God has still shown them His favor. So does God's Word in Romans 11:25–26 mean that all Jews who have ever lived will be saved in the end? No. They, like any person, have to decide to come to the Lord in repentant faith in Jesus. Since the first coming of Jesus, this has meant accepting Jesus as their Messiah, Savior, and Lord. Yes, all Jews are chosen by God, but most Jews have chosen not to embrace that calling.

This has broken the heart of our Heavenly Father who has blessed the Jews with so much. Yet like any father of a prodigal child, He still longs for them to come home in repentant faith. As we think of Jesus's story of the father with two bad boys in Luke 15:11–32, remember that He longs for both of them to come home. One does—the prodigal. One does not—the self-righteous moralist. God's love and longing, like the parent of any prodigal, does not stop. This is why when all of Israel comes to repentant faith in Jesus as Messiah, Savior, and Lord at the time of Armageddon, there will be rejoicing in heaven as never before.

Here are some things we know about Armageddon:

1. God's Word reveals Armageddon is where all history is headed. It will appear to come about under the leadership

of the Antichrist, but God is the director of the unfolding drama. The Antichrist will look unstoppable for a time. Israel will look hopeless and doomed. But God will have the final say.

2. The promise of Armageddon reminds us that Israel really is the center of the world. *Geographically,* it is the "sacred bridge" between three great continents.[3] *Historically*, Jesus came from Israel. He died on the cross and rose from the dead in Zion (Jerusalem). *Prophetically,* the Antichrist will gather troops from nations around the world to destroy Israel, that little troublemaker nation of Jews, once and for all, and Jesus will come to save His people.

3. In the end, Israel will be doubly saved. It will be saved by the Messiah physically from extinction, and it will be saved spiritually from sin and judgment through repentant faith in the Messiah, Jesus.

4. Armageddon reminds us that we don't want to be on the wrong side of history in rejecting Jesus as God's Son. That is the spirit of the Antichrist (1 John 2:22; 4:3). Being on the wrong side means becoming anti-Semitic and turning against Israel and the Jews. That is the spirit of the Antichrist. It is the mind-set of the devil. It is a mind-set that will face the judgment of God.

If you harbor feelings of resentment, prejudice, or even hatred toward Israel or Jewish people, I urge you to confess this evil in your heart and mind and repent. Ask God to cleanse you of this evil, no matter how much you feel it is justified. Remember, anti-Semitism in any form is straight from the pits of hell, and you don't want to be guilty of such evil.

At the same time, does that mean that wrongdoing on the part of Jews or Israel should be overlooked or never confronted? Absolutely not. When we love others, we are called to speak the truth to them. This means confronting evil no matter who has committed it. But hatred or prejudice against God's chosen people is clearly contrary to God's will.

19

In Those Days

Jesus Describes His Second Coming

Many people mock the second coming of Jesus, and it's understandable why. We will explore several of these reasons.

1. *False Prophets*

This may be the biggest reason. Ever since the beginning of the church, false prophets have focused on the second coming of Jesus. They are especially gifted at making gullible Christians look like idiots. This causes many skeptics to mock the whole idea.

In the early church at Thessalonica, there was great worry that Jesus had already come again and they had missed out on it. Paul wrote letters to the Thessalonians to assure them that was not the case. Obviously false prophets had sowed this seed of confusion.

ReligiousTolerance.com, to the delight of skeptics, has cataloged forty-six failed end-of-the-world predictions from AD 30 to 1920. For example, many Christians in Europe had predicted that the world would end on January 1, 1000. The date was a natural one to pick, since it was the end of the first millennium after Christ's birth. Some Christians gave all their possessions to the church in anticipation. When Christ did not come, the church did not return those gifts and understandably came under great criticism.[1]

In the 1800s, many predicted the time of Jesus's second coming. Two are particularly noteworthy. One was by Joseph Smith, founder of The Church of Jesus Christ of Latter-day Saints (the Mormons). In 1832, Smith predicted, "I prophesy in the name of the Lord God, and let it be written, the Son of Man will not come in the clouds of heaven till I am 85 years old."[2] Like all false prophets, his prediction didn't come true. He died before he turned eighty-five and, obviously, Jesus has not returned.

William Miller, who founded the Millerite movement through his study of Revelation, probably caused the biggest stir in the nineteenth century when he predicted Jesus would come between March 21, 1843, and March 21, 1844. When Jesus didn't come, his movement recalculated and said it would be October 22, 1844. When Jesus did not come, many were so disillusioned and dismayed that this became known as "The Great Disappointment" of the times.[3]

In the twentieth century, more predictions of Jesus's second coming were not realized. In 1914, 1915, 1918, 1920, 1925, and 1941, *The Watchtower Society*, published by Jehovah's Witnesses, predicted the end of the age. All of them failed, yet the cult keeps growing.

More recently, Harold Camping created quite a stir with his specific prediction of the end. Because he was a civil engineering graduate from the University of California at Berkeley, many felt God was using his genius to see biblical prophecy in a fresh light. He first predicted the second coming of Jesus to be September 6, 1994. When it did not happen, he called it a mathematical error. Then in 2010, he spread the word on more than 5,000 billboards that began to show up all around America, predicting the rapture of the church on May 21, 2011.[4] Obviously, it did not occur. Sadly, some of his followers, as in the days of William Miller, had quit their jobs and sold all their possessions to underwrite the cost of the billboards and get the word out. Amazingly, like the Millerites, he recalculated it to be October 2011, and many still believed him, only to be greatly disappointed again.

One thing is for sure, Jesus said of His second coming that "of that day and hour no one knows, not even the angels of heaven, nor the Son, but the Father alone" (Matt. 24:36). He could not be clearer. When someone predicts the time or date of Jesus's second coming, only fools take them seriously. The devil uses these false prophets to make a mockery of Christianity and Jesus's second coming.

2. *Many Jewish Rabbis teach the Jews in their synagogues to believe the second coming is a ploy, for they do not believe Jesus was the Messiah in the first place.*

Because Old Testament prophecy does not clearly differentiate between the Messiah's first and second comings, Jews believe that when the Messiah comes, it will be for the first time. An example of this lack of differentiation can be found in Isaiah 9:6. It moves from Jesus's first coming to His second coming within that one verse. This happens repeatedly in the Messianic prophecy of the old covenant, so it is understandable why Jewish scholars reject Jesus and do not believe He fulfilled the prophecies.

3. *It's been more than two thousand years and Jesus has not returned.*

God's Word speaks to this in 2 Peter:

> Know this first of all, that *in the last days mockers will come with their mocking*, following after their own lusts, and saying, "Where is the promise of His coming? For ever since the fathers fell asleep, all continues just as it was from the beginning of creation." (2 Pet. 3:3–4, emphasis added)

There is no doubt that many in the early church felt Jesus's second coming was imminent. Paul's letters attest to this. Now that it has been more than two thousand years, the skepticism has only grown.

Jesus's Prophecy of His Second Coming

Jesus clearly taught about His second coming. Matthew 24 and 25 offer all kinds of insight surrounding it. Matthew 24:29 describes what actually precedes it:

> But immediately after the tribulation of those days THE SUN WILL BE DARKENED, AND THE MOON WILL NOT GIVE ITS LIGHT, AND THE STARS WILL FALL from the sky, and the powers of the heavens will be shaken.

This will come at the end of the Great Tribulation. We've seen how the Antichrist will consolidate his one-world government so he can unify the world around worshiping him. Yet Jesus said those days will be days of Great Tribulation (Matt. 24:15–28). They will be very difficult days for the Jews and any who become followers of Christ in the Great Tribulation. Many false prophets and false Christs will add to the confusion of those days (verse 24).

Perhaps most frightening, however, will be the cataclysmic events that will occur in the cosmos around the time of Jesus's second coming, as described in Matthew 24:29. The sun will grow dark. This will obviously cause the moon to no longer be seen, and remnants of stars and asteroids will be pounding the earth. If you think the world appears to be falling into chaos today because of world events, just think of the chaos, fear, and terror this will create. All hell will be breaking loose even in the heavens.

Thus, at the end of the Great Tribulation when the Antichrist has gathered his millions of troops at Armageddon to destroy Israel once and for all, Jesus will appear in the clouds as an answer to the prayers of the Jews pleading for God to send the Messiah and save them.

We've seen how this will lead to nationwide repentance on behalf of the Jews and Israel, but how will the rest of the world respond?

> And then the sign of the Son of Man will appear in the sky, and then all the tribes of the earth will mourn, and they will see the Son of Man coming on the clouds of the sky with power and great glory. (Matt. 24:30)

So all the tribes on the face of the earth will mourn. Why? Well, by that time the church will have taken the gospel of

Christ to every people group on the face of the earth. That doesn't mean every person in those people groups will be saved. In most cases, the majority of each people group will reject the gift of salvation God offers in Christ. Yet some from every tribe and people group will have accepted Christ through faith as their Savior and Lord.

The mourning from every tribe and people group will occur among those who have never responded in repentant faith to follow Jesus. They will be like the Jews, who will realize they deserve to face judgment for their sins. But unlike the Jews, there is no indication they come to repentant faith. They simply mourn knowing they are facing the judgment they deserve.

When Jesus comes for His church in the rapture, it will be a time of great joy and celebration that leads to the ultimate destination wedding of Jesus (the groom) and His bride (the church) in heaven. Yet at Jesus's second coming, it will be a day of great mourning on the earth, for it will be a day of judgment. This is what the Bible calls the Great Day of the Lord. It will be a day of reckoning for those who have followed the Antichrist rather than Jesus.

The Revelation on Jesus's Second Coming

Revelation 19:11–21 describes a sobering picture of what this day will look like. It is not a pretty picture.

Judgment Day

> Mine eyes have seen the glory of the coming of the Lord;
> He is trampling out the vintage where the grapes of
>   wrath are stored;

He hath loosed the fateful lightning of His terrible swift
   sword:
His truth is marching on. ~Julia Ward Howe

Most Americans will recognize the first stanza of "The
Battle Hymn of the Republic." Howe wrote these words after
she attended a review of Union troops and joined in singing
the new soldiers' song, "John Brown's Body," a song about
a man who had been hanged in his efforts to free the slaves.
She felt the tune should have better words.[5] Her verse was
first published in *The Atlantic Monthly* in February 1862 and
quickly became a popular song of the Union soldiers who
saw themselves in the noble cause of serving the Union and
defeating the treacherous, slave-holding rebels of the South.
She used the words of Revelation 19:11–19 that describe
Jesus's second coming because she thought their cause was
so great. Stanzas 2–5, unlike the first stanza, describe the
nobility of the Union troops and their righteous cause.

I've listed the first stanza because it is a very good summary
of what Revelation 19 says about Jesus's second coming.
It will be a day of reckoning on the unrighteous who have
been swept up in the hypnotic spell of the Antichrist. It will
be Judgment Day:

And I saw heaven opened, and behold, a white horse. (Rev.
19:11a)

Jesus appearing on a white horse symbolizes the coming of
a conquering king. Alexander the Great had his great horse,
Bucephalus. It was a head taller than any other horse and
untamable. Alexander stunned the royal Macedonian court
of his father by mounting and taming Bucephalus when he

was just twelve years old. His father was so moved that he exclaimed, "O my son, look thee out a kingdom equal to and worthy of thyself, for Macedonia is too little for thee."[6] Alexander rode the horse into every battle and region of the world he conquered. Only Alexander could ride him. What a majestic sight it had to be!

Yet it was nothing like the sight Jesus will be on His great white horse when He returns in the clouds. Instantly, the world will know He has come as the conquering king. The world and the troops gathered at Armageddon will be terrified. It will be the most abrupt societal change in all of history. One moment the Antichrist will appear unstoppable— mighty and great. Then in the blink of an eye, he will seem small and helpless at the sight of Jesus in the sky.

Look at what God's Word tells us of this sight—what it tells us of Jesus.

Jesus Returns as Conquering King

And He who sat on it is called Faithful and True. (Rev. 19:11b)

Jesus is called faithful and true. He is the only man who has been perfectly faithful in fulfilling God's will. He is true. Jesus himself said He is the truth (John 14:6).

The Judge

Jesus's second coming is about judgment and waging war. His judgment is righteous. He is the only one who knows the full story of each of our lives and all of the earth. His judgments are true and right. Many people today—even in the church—find it offensive to think of Jesus as a judge, for the majority in American churches tend to be practical

Universalists. As we discussed in chapter 9, a Universalist believes there are many ways to God. They love the idea of heaven but don't really believe a loving God would send anyone to hell, especially their nice and kind neighbor who doesn't believe in Jesus. Oh, maybe a Hitler or Osama bin Laden or "women who didn't vote for Hillary,"[7] but very few are considered bad enough. Universalists would rarely admit they are Unitarians, but they have more in common with Unitarianism than biblical Christianity.

Jesus himself said in His ministry:

> For not even the Father judges anyone, but He has given all judgment to the Son, so that all will honor the Son even as they honor the Father. He who does not honor the Son does not honor the Father who sent Him. . . . For just as the Father has life in Himself, even so He gave to the Son also to have life in Himself; and He gave Him authority to execute judgment, because He is the Son of Man. (John 5:22–23, 26–27)

When Jesus comes again, that picture will be clear.

Waging War

And in righteousness He judges and wages war. (Rev. 19:11c)

Jesus will come not only as a righteous and just judge, but He will also come to wage war with the Antichrist and all of his followers. It will be the ultimate visible spiritual warfare.

His Eyes

His eyes are a flame of fire. (Rev. 19:12a)

In the movies *Braveheart* and *The Patriot*, Mel Gibson's eyes give us an idea of what it is like to have eyes like "a flame of fire" as he rallies the troops in a righteous cause against the British—always the British.

I remember as a boy watching the close-up shots of Dick Butkus, the ferocious linebacker for the Chicago Bears. What wild eyes he had! If I had seen those eyes staring at me from the offensive line, I would have wanted to stay out of his way. Mike Singletary, another great Chicago Bears linebacker, also had incredibly intense eyes. Those players were going to war. No one could stop them. No one stood a chance. Jesus's eyes will be like that. He will be outraged when He sees the massive gathering of troops under the Antichrist that have come to destroy the people He loves—His people, Israel. He will be on a mission to save them.

His Crown

On His head are many diadems. (Rev. 19:12b)

Jesus will have a glorious crown on His head. What this really looks like is beyond my imagination, but it will be awesome. One thing is for sure—everyone will know that He has returned as King, Messiah, and Lord.

His Unknown Name

He has a name written on Him which no one knows except Himself. (Rev. 19:12c)

All through the ages, many have speculated about what this name is. Some have suggested that Exodus 3:14 provides the answer. When God appeared to Moses in the burning bush, Moses asked Him what he should tell the sons of Israel when they wanted to know the name of God the Father who sent him. God replied, "I AM WHO I AM"; and He said, "Thus you shall say to the sons of Israel, 'I AM has sent me to you.'"

This is my conclusion about that name . . . *I don't know!* How can anyone know? Only Jesus knows.

His Clothing

He is clothed with a robe dipped in blood. (Rev. 19:13a)

His robe will have been dipped in blood—the blood He shed at the cross for all humankind. All through history His blood has been a reminder of His love and offer of forgiveness. It will be a reminder of the price He paid on the cross. Yet now, after much of humankind has stubbornly rejected His love, that blood will be a reminder of why His judgment is just.

His Title

And on His robe and on His thigh He has a name written, "KING OF KINGS, AND LORD OF LORDS." (Rev. 19:16)

He will be an awesome sight, and His followers will be in awe—glorious awe. For the sight of Him and all of His holiness and goodness will be magnificent. Jesus is unlike every king on earth. He is greater than any king or emperor or president who has ever lived.

His Name

His name is called The Word of God. (Rev. 19:13b)

The apostle John makes this clear in his introduction to Jesus in the Gospel of John:

> In the beginning was the Word, and the Word was with God, and the Word was God. He was in the beginning with God. All things came into being through Him, and apart from Him nothing came into being that has come into being. . . . And the Word became flesh, and dwelt among us, and we saw His glory, glory as of the only begotten from the Father, full of grace and truth. (John 1:1–3, 14)

Scripture is the special revelation of the written Word of God. Jesus is the Word of God that became flesh so that we can see God in the flesh. We are directly dependent on God's special revelation (the written Word of God) to have the perfect picture of His ultimate revelation of Himself—Jesus, the Word of God. Those who dismiss any part of Scripture as not being God's Word begin to see an incomplete picture of the Word of God—Jesus. All through Jesus's ministry, He fulfilled the written Word of God. He upheld it while showing us the right interpretation of God's written Word. He came to show us what it means and how to live it. He teaches us to believe it is true.

His Army—Who Will It Be?

> And the armies which are in heaven, clothed in fine linen, white and clean, were following Him on white horses. (Rev. 19:14)

Who are these armies from heaven? Could they be angels? Maybe, but we can only speculate. And what about Old Testament saints—those looking for the coming Messiah through faith? How could they be left out? Could they be the martyrs who died for their faith in the Great Tribulation? Certainly they are heroes in the kingdom of God. We'll see in a future chapter how that is the case.

Yet as we've seen in our study of the rapture, one group is indisputable as being part of His army of heaven that returns with Him—the church. The description of this army "clothed in fine linen, white and clean" is just like the description of the bride of Christ (the church) that will have been raptured earlier by Jesus for the ultimate destination wedding in heaven. Revelation 19:8 tells of the clothing of Christ's bride for that heavenly feast. We don't know how many Christians have lived since Jesus's death, burial, and resurrection, but almost two billion people claim to be Christian today. I realize many of these are cultural Christians who are not really in the body of Christ, but all the Christians who have ever lived would still have to be in the billions. One thing about warfare and military might—no army wants to be outnumbered. The forces of the Antichrist gathered at Armageddon will suddenly be overwhelmed with terror at the sight of Christ's army of billions appearing with Him in the sky. What an overwhelming sight it will be!

Christ and His Army's Weapons

From His mouth comes a sharp sword, so that with it He may strike down the nations, and He will rule them with a rod of iron; and He treads the wine press of the fierce wrath of God, the Almighty. (Rev. 19:15)

His army will be unarmed. No weapons. Zilch. There will be no need, for Christ is the only one armed. It is called the sharp sword of His mouth. Obviously, this is the Word of

God. God uses this word "sword" to describe our greatest offensive weapon in spiritual warfare:

> The sword of the Spirit, which is the word of God. (Eph. 6:17b)

This battle will be over with a word. When Jesus gives the word, the Antichrist and his troops will be destroyed. Won't that be a sight! The supposedly invincible armies of the Antichrist armed to the teeth with all the latest weapons and technology will stand no chance against the ultimate weapon—the Word of God.

Jesus will strike them with a word of the wrath of God, the Almighty, and begin to rule all the earth with a rod of iron. This will be another example of how Jesus, as Messiah, is the fulfillment of Old Testament prophecy: "You shall break them with a rod of iron, You shall shatter them like earthenware" (Ps. 2:9).

The Judgment

> Then I saw an angel standing in the sun, and he cried out with a loud voice, saying to all the birds which fly in midheaven, "Come, assemble for the great supper of God, so that you may eat the flesh of kings and the flesh of commanders and the flesh of mighty men and the flesh of horses and of those who sit on them and the flesh of all men, both free men and slaves, and small and great."
>
> And I saw the beast and the kings of the earth and their armies assembled to make war against Him who sat on the horse and against His army. (Rev. 19:17–19)

This passage does not paint a pretty picture. It shows the vultures and the buzzards and the scavenger birds rounded up by the Word of God to prepare for a great feast. That feast will be the flesh of kings and generals, soldiers, horses, and powerful and powerless men in the Antichrist's army. They will all be killed with a word. Birds will be drawn from Europe, Asia, and Africa to this central point of all the earth—Israel—that is the crossroad of these three continents:

> And the beast was seized, and with him the false prophet who performed the signs in his presence, by which he deceived those who had received the mark of the beast and those who worshiped his image; these two were thrown alive into the lake of fire which burns with brimstone. And the rest were killed with the sword which came from the mouth of Him who sat on the horse, and all the birds were filled with their flesh. (Rev. 19:20–21)

The Antichrist (the beast) and his false prophet, who will have the supernatural power of the Evil One that empowered them to deceive many, will both be cast into hell. Then the millions of soldiers under the Antichrist at Armageddon will be killed.

It is not a pretty picture for the lost, but for those in Jesus's army—the true church—it will be a day of great relief and gratitude. At last the Antichrist will be destroyed and the earth no longer deceived by him. At last evil on the earth will be subdued. The day of reckoning will have come.

Do you remember the day you heard Osama bin Laden had been killed by American Special Forces in Pakistan? Do you remember the sense of relief? Well, that feeling will be miniscule compared to what the church and the redeemed Jews will feel after suffering so long at the hands of evil.

When we pray, "Your kingdom come. Your will be done, on earth as it is in heaven" (Matt. 6:10), we are longing for

God's kingdom and righteousness here on earth. On that day, our prayer will be realized.

So what in the world is Jesus waiting on? There is so much evil in the world today. Why doesn't He come now? God's Word gives the answer:

> The Lord is not slow about His promise, as some count slowness, but is patient toward you, not wishing for any to perish but for all to come to repentance. (2 Pet. 3:9)

The mercy and grace of God desires for no one to perish. He longs for everyone to be redeemed, to become children of God through faith in His Son. Yes, He knows most will not, but His heart's desire is for all to be saved.

If you are reading this book and are not sure of your salvation or whether you would return with Christ as part of His army, may you trust Christ through repentant faith today. God, in His mercy and grace, has delayed the second coming of His Son for you. He loves you that much. He sent His Son the first time to pay the penalty for your sins. He came to conquer sin and death. He delays sending Him the second time because of you—He doesn't want you or anyone else to perish physically or spiritually. May you come to repentant faith today.

And if you are a Christian, may you live with the anticipation and hope of Jesus coming again. May you make the most of the time you have here on earth in sharing the good news of salvation through Christ with those who need to know Him. No calling is greater. No purpose is more important for the follower of Jesus.

But there is more to look forward to in that great and glorious day.

20

The Touchdown

Jesus Returns to His City

Nothing excites a football fan more than when their team executes a Hail Mary touchdown on the last play of the game to win. That may be the ultimate euphoria in football.

Yet, as exciting as that is, it doesn't compare to the excitement Israel will feel when Jesus and His team, the church, touchdown at His second coming. It will seem that Israel's situation is hopeless. The mighty army of the Antichrist will be poised to exterminate Israel once and for all. Then in the moment when defeat seems sure, Israel will cry out to God to send the Messiah to save them—and He will.

Jesus will appear in the clouds and with a word cast the Antichrist and his false prophet into hell and bring judgment on their millions of soldiers gathered at Armageddon. He will save Israel from extermination and rescue His people from sin and death and hell through His amazing grace. According to Zechariah 14:3,

Then the LORD will go forth and fight against those nations, as when He fights on a day of battle.

Then He will touch down on the Mount of Olives that is to the east of Jerusalem. The prophet Zechariah describes it this way:

> In that day His feet will stand on the Mount of Olives, which is in front of Jerusalem on the east; and the Mount of Olives will be split in its middle from east to west by a very large valley, so that half of the mountain will move toward the north and the other half toward the south. (Zech. 14:4)

What a celebration it will be! The Jews of Israel will be ecstatic. The Jews around the world who see it on television will be weeping for joy. And at last the Jews and the church will be one in celebration of Jesus, as Messiah and Lord, touching down on the Mount of Olives. What a day of victory!

The original guide on my Bible study tours to Israel was a God-fearing Jew named Mati. In regard to when the Messiah comes and touches down on the Mount of Olives, he used to say, "If He comes for the first time, you'll need to apologize to me. If He comes for the second time, then I'll apologize to you." Bible-believing Jews and Christians agree on where the Messiah will touch down when He comes because of Zechariah 14:4—and it will be equally clear to both that the Messiah has come for a second time. He will return exactly as the angels said He would—from the very spot where He ascended to heaven forty days after His resurrection. As His disciples stood with Him on the Mount of Olives that day, this is what occurred:

> And after He had said these things, He was lifted up while they were looking on, and a cloud received Him out of their

sight. And as they were gazing intently into the sky while He was going, behold, two men in white clothing stood beside them. They also said, "Men of Galilee, why do you stand looking into the sky? This Jesus, who has been taken up from you into heaven, will come in just the same way as you have watched Him go into heaven."

Then they returned to Jerusalem from the mount called Olivet, which is near Jerusalem, a Sabbath day's journey away. (Acts 1:9–12)

This is why I love having a worship service on the Mount of Olives. Few places on the earth are more important to the past and the future than the Mount of Olives. It was from there that Jesus descended as He entered Jerusalem on what we call Palm Sunday. It was from there that He ascended to heaven. And it will be the ultimate celebration in history in the future when He touches down there when He comes again.

At that time, a massive earthquake will transform the topographic landscape around Jerusalem. As Zechariah writes, "The Mount of Olives will be split in its middle from east to west." This will form a large valley as half the mountain moves to the north and half to the south.

Zechariah writes of how the Jews will have fled from the area during the Great Tribulation and then Jesus will come:

You will flee by the valley of My mountains, for the valley of the mountains will reach to Azel; yes, you will flee just as you fled before the earthquake in the days of Uzziah king of Judah. Then the LORD, my God, will come, and all the holy ones with Him! (Zech. 14:5)

Zechariah 14:6–7 provides insight regarding this cataclysmic event:

In that day there will be no light; the luminaries will dwindle.
For it will be a unique day which is known to the LORD,
neither day nor night, but it will come about that at evening
time there will be light.

In Jesus's teaching on His second coming in Matthew
24:29, He spoke of the sun and moon darkening before He
comes. Well after He has arrived, there will be no more need
for the light of the sun and moon, because Jesus Christ, the
ultimate light, will illuminate all the earth.

This shouldn't surprise the student of the Bible. The very
first page is a record of God creating the world: "Then God
said, 'Let there be light'; and there was light" (Gen. 1:3). This
was the first day, and the sun and moon were not created until
the fourth day. How could there have been light? Jesus is the
Light of the World—literally and spiritually.

Peter, James, and John had a preview of this brilliant
light when Jesus was transfigured in front of them on what
is today called the Mount of Transfiguration (Matt. 17:2).
When Jesus returns, His light—the light of His glorified,
resurrected body—will bring light to all, and there will be
no more night.

Revelation 21:22–26 describes Jesus as "the light" even
more vividly:

I saw no temple in it, for the Lord God the Almighty and
the Lamb are its temple. And the city has no need of the
sun or of the moon to shine on it, for the glory of God has
illumined it, and its lamp is the Lamb. The nations will walk
by its light, and the kings of the earth will bring their glory
into it. In the daytime (for there will be no night there) its
gates will never be closed; and they will bring the glory and
the honor of the nations into it.

Because of the giant earthquake when Jesus touches down, another amazing geological event will occur:

> And in that day living waters will flow out of Jerusalem, half of them toward the eastern sea and the other half toward the western sea; it will be in summer as well as in winter. (Zech. 14:8)

What is the sea to the east? What is the sea to the west? How can water flow out of Jerusalem as if it is an elevated city? The sea to the west is the Mediterranean Sea. The sea to the east is the Dead Sea. There is no life in the Dead Sea today. Yet Ezekiel prophesied in the sixth century BC that one day the waters of the Dead Sea would become fresh and teeming with life:

> Then he said to me, "These waters go out toward the eastern region and go down into the Arabah; then they go toward the sea, being made to flow into the sea, and the waters of the sea become fresh. It will come about that every living creature which swarms in every place where the river goes, will live. And there will be very many fish, for these waters go there and the others become fresh; so everything will live where the river goes. And it will come about that fishermen will stand beside it; from Engedi to Eneglaim there will be a place for the spreading of nets. Their fish will be according to their kinds, like the fish of the Great Sea, very many. (Ezek. 47:8–10)

Life in the Dead Sea is impossible today. The salt and mineral content is about ten times greater than the Atlantic or Pacific Oceans because it has no outlet. The Jordan River flows into it but stops there. Yet when Jesus touches down on the Mount of Olives and the massive geological shift occurs from the earthquake, the Dead Sea will be teeming with life, for water will then flow in and out of it.

Jesus Enters Jerusalem to Reign

> And the LORD will be king over all the earth; in that day the LORD will be the only one, and His name the only one. (Zech. 14:9)

At Jesus's second coming He will appear in the clouds and touch down on the Mount of Olives. He will ride His white horse up to the Eastern Gate to enter Jerusalem. The leaders of His army, the church, along with the leaders of redeemed Israel, will be a part of His procession. Then He will reign from the throne of David in Jerusalem as Samuel the prophet foretold thousands of years ago:

> Your house and your kingdom shall endure before Me forever; your throne shall be established forever. (2 Sam. 7:16)

Biblical Jews are clear on the fact that when the Messiah comes, He will reign from the throne of David in Jerusalem. But there is a problem.

Photo credit: Austin Smith.

Eastern Gate.

198

The Eastern Gate into Jerusalem has been sealed over for hundreds of years. This occurred because the Muslim ruler of that day heard that the Jews believed their Messiah would enter Jerusalem from the east, from the Mount of Olives, and seek to reign over Jerusalem. So he had the gate sealed. This means it would be impossible to enter Jerusalem through those gates—the seal is fifteen to sixteen feet thick.[1]

What is astounding is the prophet Ezekiel foretold of this about two thousand years before it occurred:

> Then He brought me back by the way of the outer gate of the sanctuary, which faces the east; and it was shut. The LORD said to me, "This gate shall be shut; it shall not be opened, and no one shall enter by it, for the LORD God of Israel has entered by it; therefore it shall be shut. As for the prince, he shall sit in it as prince to eat bread before the LORD; he shall enter by way of the porch of the gate and shall go out by the same way." (Ezek. 44:1–3)

In other words, Ezekiel was saying that at some point in the future the Eastern Gate in Jerusalem would be shut and not be opened until the Messiah comes through it to enter Jerusalem.

So how will it be opened? Remember that dramatic earthquake that will occur when Jesus touches down on the Mount of Olives? Maybe that will open the gate. However, Jesus's resurrected body was not hindered by walls and matter. He appeared and disappeared when the disciples were in hiding behind locked doors. That poor Muslim ruler who sealed the gate was simply playing into the hands of biblical prophecy and didn't even know it.

When Jesus Will Reign over All the Earth

It is fascinating to see how the Old Testament prophets spoke the Word of God under the inspiration of the Holy Spirit and often had no idea how all this prophecy would flesh out. God led them to say it and write it, and it is so. We know they didn't understand how it would all work out because they never spoke of the Messiah coming twice. They just spoke of the Messiah's coming. (As we have seen, this is one reason Jews of the first century and Jews of the twenty-first century reject Jesus as Messiah. He did not fulfill all the prophecy concerning the Messiah.)

The most well-known verse of the book of Isaiah is Isaiah 9:6:

> For a child will be born to us, a son will be given to us; And the government will rest on His shoulders; and His name will be called Wonderful Counselor, Mighty God, Eternal Father, Prince of Peace. (Isa. 9:6)

This verse in Handel's *Messiah* is usually sung at Christmastime, but most of the prophecy was not fulfilled in Jesus's lifetime. In fact, only the first part of verse 6—"A child will be born to us, a son will be given to us"—was fulfilled. Verses 6b–7 are yet to be fulfilled. Jesus didn't lead a government of peace over all the world from the throne of David as the Prince of Peace. Christians know all this refers to the Messiah's second coming.

Zechariah's prophecy also offers another example of a lack of distinction between the Messiah's first and second comings. Zechariah 9:9 describes what Jesus would do on Palm Sunday. And verse 10 is obviously speaking of Jesus's second coming, yet this verse is often ignored:

Rejoice greatly, O daughter of Zion! Shout in triumph, O daughter of Jerusalem! Behold, your king is coming to you; he is just and endowed with salvation, humble, and mounted on a donkey, even on a colt, the foal of a donkey [Palm Sunday].

I will cut off the chariot from Ephraim and the horse from Jerusalem; and the bow of war will be cut off. And He will speak peace to the nations; and His dominion will be from sea to sea, and from the River to the ends of the earth [Jesus's second coming]. (Zech. 9:9–10)

Just like Isaiah, Zechariah moves from Jesus's first coming to His second coming in just two verses. Yet the prophets are clear that when the Messiah comes, He will have dominion from sea to sea. He will reign over all the earth, and at last there will be peace on earth.

In That Day, Jesus's Name Will Be the Name above All Names

His name the only one. (Zech. 14:9b)

There no longer will be other religions on earth. There will be no more Islam, no more Hinduism, no more Buddhism, and no more cults. There will be just one Lord, one faith, one name above all names—and it will be Jesus.

21

Three Great Feasts

The Annual Celebration of His Coming

Obviously, Jesus's second coming will be the climactic event in all of history. His incarnation in Bethlehem showed us God in the flesh. His death on the cross was the ultimate and final sacrifice that secured our forgiveness and salvation from sin and hell. His resurrection gave us victory over death. His ascension to heaven from the Mount of Olives began his reign at the right hand of the Father, where he is today. Yet His second coming will begin His reign over all the earth. Just as Christmas and Easter help Christians focus on His birth and His resurrection, His second coming will be an annual celebration in all the earth.

It will occur during the Feast of Booths (the Feast of Tabernacles) that occurs in late September or early October each year. Tabernacles is the third great Jewish feast that Jews are called to celebrate each year:

Then it will come about that any who are left of all the nations that went against Jerusalem will go up from year to year to worship the King, the LORD of hosts, and to celebrate the Feast of Booths. And it will be that whichever of the families of the earth does not go up to Jerusalem to worship the King, the LORD of hosts, there will be no rain on them. (Zech. 14:16–17)

The nations that opposed Israel under the Antichrist (that would be all the nations) will be required to go to Jerusalem each year during the Feast of Booths (or Tabernacles) to worship King Jesus. Obviously, all seven billion people will not be able to go to Jerusalem at the same time, but every nation will send their representatives to honor and worship King Jesus.

Why?

It will be a time of proclamation and teaching about this "new world order." Micah the prophet writes:

And it will come about in the last days that the mountain of the house of the Lord will be established as the chief of the mountains. It will be raised above the hills, and the peoples will stream to it. Many nations will come and say, "Come and let us go up to the mountain of the Lord and to the house of the God of Jacob, that He may teach us about His ways and that we may walk in His paths." For from Zion will go forth the law, even the word of the Lord from Jerusalem. (Mic. 4:1–2)

Jesus will teach all the nations His ways, how to walk in His path, and what is right and wrong. Nations that do not send representatives to worship and learn from Jesus will have famine over the whole year to come.

Yet why during the Feast of Tabernacles? Obviously, it will be related to the timing of Jesus's second coming. What's interesting is that of the three great annual Jewish feasts, Tabernacles is the only one with no Christian parallel.

Passover

Passover that leads into the Feast of Unleavened Bread has a Christian parallel in Jesus's crucifixion. It was no accident that Jesus, the Lamb of God, was crucified and shed His blood on the cross to die in our place during that great feast. It is the time when Jewish people remember how the Hebrew families were told to sacrifice an unblemished lamb and spread the blood of the lamb on the doorposts of their houses. When the Angel of Death and Judgment passed over Egypt to kill the firstborn of every Egyptian household, it would see the blood of the lamb on the household of faith and pass over that house, sparing the household from God's judgment of death.

This led to Egypt's setting the children of Israel free from slavery through the shed blood of the lamb. It is the perfect parallel to what the Lamb of God did for us on the cross, setting us free from slavery and bondage to sin. Jesus died in our place to save us from judgment and death. Passover always occurs in early spring (late March or early to mid-April). Good Friday and Easter should always fall during Passover, yet sadly the early church fathers used the ancient Roman calendar concerning spring to set that annual observance.

Pentecost

The second great annual feast of the Jews is Pentecost. It occurs in late May or early June on our calendar. The Jews celebrate Pentecost for two reasons: (1) it is a celebration of the firstfruits of the harvest of all the crops, and (2) it is a celebration of when Moses received the law of God on Mount Sinai in the beginning days of the nation of Israel.

For Christians, Pentecost is when the church began. The Holy Spirit descended on Jesus's disciples during Pentecost when Jews from all around the world had gathered in Jerusalem to celebrate both the firstfruits of harvest and the receiving of the law in the beginning days of their nation.

When Peter stood to preach during Pentecost, three thousand souls were saved and baptized that day to begin the church. They were the "firstfruits" of lives that would be saved through the preaching of the gospel by the church. Pentecost and Passover have very clear Christian parallels.

Tabernacles

Of the three great annual feasts of the Jews, Tabernacles has no Christian parallel. Yet the Feast of Tabernacles or Booths recalls the days when the Jews wandered in the wilderness for forty years because of their hardheadedness in refusing to claim the land God had promised them. Moses, their leader, sent in twelve spies to see the land and glean insight on what they would face in claiming it. Most of the spies said there was no way they could do it; the people there were too great and powerful. Yet two of the spies, Joshua and Caleb, believed God and His power would be sufficient to claim the Promised Land for Israel. Sadly, the people believed the majority report and rejected God's will. God punished them by making them wander in the wilderness for forty years until the whole generation older than twenty years old died off, except for Moses, Joshua, and Caleb. Because of their faith, they were allowed to live.

How fitting for Tabernacles to be the time to celebrate Jesus's second coming as the Jewish Messiah. To this very day, the majority of Jews have rejected the salvation found in Christ as they spiritually wander in the wilderness—blind to the light and truth and salvation in Jesus.

How fitting it will be for Jesus to come around Tabernacles because it is the feast that celebrates the end of the harvest in early fall. At that point, the work of the church in the harvesting of souls will be complete. In light of Zechariah 14:16–17, all this makes sense.

It is also fascinating that all good Jews who were able were expected to travel to Jerusalem during the three great Jewish feasts. Jerusalem would sometimes swell to ten times its normal size. So it is perfectly consistent that the Lord would require delegates from every nation on earth to travel to Jerusalem where "EVERY KNEE WILL BOW . . . and . . . every tongue will confess that Jesus Christ is Lord" (Phil. 2:10–11).

Passover and the cross. Pentecost and the beginning of the harvest of souls at the beginning of the church. And Tabernacles, celebrating the end of the harvest of souls by the church, and the end of spiritual wandering by the Jews of Israel. It is fascinating to consider. Yet only the Lord knows when it will be. One thing is for sure: there are no accidents in God's timing. All that happens in the old covenant can only be fully understood in Jesus and the new covenant. All of the old covenant is a preparation for the coming of Jesus.

22

Your Kingdom Come

The Millennial Reign

When Christ comes for His church in the rapture, it will be a glorious time of joy and celebration. When Christ comes with His church at His second coming, it will be a time of judgment on evil.

Revelation 19:17–21 describes how the Antichrist and the false prophet will be cast into hell and the millions in the Antichrist's army gathered at Armageddon will be killed. But that is not the only judgment that will occur. The ultimate instigator of evil and rebellion against God will be cast into hell as well. Revelation 20:1–3 tells us who this is:

> Then I saw an angel coming down from heaven, holding the key of the abyss and a great chain in his hand. And he laid hold of the dragon, the serpent of old, who is the devil and Satan, and bound him for a thousand years; and he threw

him into the abyss, and shut it and sealed it over him, so that he would not deceive the nations any longer, until the thousand years were completed; after these things he must be released for a short time.

The devil is described with four different names.

1. The *dragon*: Dragons are symbolic of ultimate cruelty. They are seen as terrifying killing machines. The devil is described as the dragon in Revelation 12:9.

2. The *serpent of old* goes all the way back to the beginning in Genesis 3, when it was just Adam and Eve in the Garden of Eden. Sometime before this, the devil had been cast out of heaven for trying to usurp God. He appeared to Eve as the tempter in the form of a snake. I hate snakes. I'm afraid of snakes. Poisonous or not. Big or small. Alive or dead. They give me the creeps. I think it goes all the way back to the Garden of Eden.

   Yet before man's fall into original sin, snakes must not have been frightening at all. There were no wild animals. All of creation was in harmony with one another. Evidently, there was something alluring and attractive in a snake that aroused Eve's curiosity. The serpent of old was the ultimate tempter.

3. The *devil* means "accuser." The word in Greek is *diabolos*. It is the same word that is used for a malicious gossip or false witness or slanderer. You want to be like the devil? You can be—every time you gossip and slander and falsely accuse someone. One reason the devil is the ultimate jerk is that he tempts us to do something wrong and then when we do it, he begins to accuse us

of doing wrong. He heaps guilt and shame on us when it was he who tempted us to fall into sin.

When I was in the third grade, there was a cute little gal in my class who behaved this way. She would tempt me to pass a note to another student in class or do something the teacher had told us not to do. Because she was so cute and I wanted to please her, I would do it, and then when I did, she would shout to the teacher, "Bryant is passing notes in class!" She was like a little devil. Maybe you have known people like this.

4. *Satan* means "the enemy." He is the enemy of God. He is the enemy of man. He wants to destroy our lives. This is in contrast to Jesus, who came to save our lives and give us life abundantly (John 10:10).

When Jesus comes again, He will bind the devil and cast him into the abyss.

The Abyss

An abyss is a bottomless pit. Satan will be thrown into a place where there is no escape. Abyss is another symbolic term for hell.

I've had the privilege of scuba diving at Grand Cayman several times. About a mile offshore is a wall where depths are estimated to drop from fifty or sixty feet to more than two thousand feet. As we've dived around the top of that wall, I've looked down into the darkness of the deep many times and thought if something went wrong and we had an equipment failure, it would be like falling into an abyss. Our bodies would never be found. No one would be able to get to us. It is a haunting sight.

Binding the Devil?

I've been in prayer with people before at an important ministry event, and someone has asked God to "bind the devil." I know the intention of their prayers is for God to keep the devil from disrupting the ministry or worship event in a way that takes the focus off Jesus. Yet the devil will not be truly bound until Jesus comes again and casts him into the abyss of hell. No longer will he be able to tempt us and accuse us and destroy us. No longer will he be able to distract us from focusing on Jesus. All that will be over. Good riddance to the ultimate evil influence in all of creation.

The Devil Will Be Imprisoned in Hell for One Thousand Years

God plans to keep the devil bound in hell for one thousand years. Then He will release the devil for a short time. That is puzzling. Why in the world would God do this? I realize it's not my place to question God's plan (a gross understatement), but this one is troubling. Why not just keep the devil in hell forever, where he deserves to be?

Believe it or not, there is a reason. In the millennial reign of Christ, life on earth will finally be as it ought to be—a place of peace, justice, compassion, love, and unity. But not everyone will have given their hearts and devotion to Christ. Remember, He will rule "with a rod of iron" (Rev. 19:15). There will be no rebellion against God as there is today. Yet millions will be born in that thousand-year period, and all will have the same decision to make about Jesus: *Do I trust Him with all my heart so as to voluntarily surrender my will to Him? Or do I simply obey under His new world order because I have to?*

At the end of Jesus's thousand-year reign, the devil will be released by Christ from the prison of hell. He will lead a rebellion of nations against Christ and His reign. This rebellion will reveal the true hearts of everyone. Some will have hearts of rebellion against Christ, and some will have hearts for Christ:

> When the thousand years are completed, Satan will be released from his prison, and will come out to deceive the nations which are in the four corners of the earth, Gog and Magog, to gather them together for the war; the number of them is like the sand of the seashore. And they came up on the broad plain of the earth and surrounded the camp of the saints and the beloved city. (Rev. 20:7–9a)

After this, the Lord will strike them with fire from heaven, and the devil will be eternally cast into hell. All humankind who has not been spiritually born as a child of God through faith in Christ will be cast into hell with the devil in the final judgment. Revelation 20:11–15 describes this.

At that point, all humankind will be separated into two groups: the saved and the judged. Which group will you be in?

Is Christ's Millennial Reign on Earth an Actual One Thousand Years?

Some feel that one thousand is a symbolic number—symbolic of eternity, of a complete period of time. After all, so much of Revelation is symbolic imagery. Why would this be different?

Yet one thousand years is repeated six times in Revelation 20:2–7. It seems to me that God is making a strong point. It is not a complete period of time as many believe, for it will be followed by one final rebellion and one final judgment of all humankind. For that reason, it just makes sense that this is an actual one thousand years.

There are four major theological views of Christ's millennial reign on earth.

1. The *premillennial view*. Whether you believe the rapture of the church happens before Jesus's second coming or that those events occur at the same time, this view simply trusts that when Christ comes again, He will reign over the earth for an actual one thousand years. This view is clearly taught in Revelation 19–20. Most evangelical Christians believe this.

2. The *postmillennial view*. This is largely out of favor today but was extremely popular at the end of the nineteenth century and the beginning of the twentieth century. It is a much more optimistic view of history. Since the church is leading people to Christ and working for social justice and righteousness, one day the earth will be prepared and ready for Christ to come and reign. This view believes that the world is gradually getting better and better. In this view, the one thousand years are a symbolic period of time and the church is to be busy in well-doing to hasten the day.

   Whatever you do, if you believe this view, don't watch the news. Don't read the news in the paper or on your tablet or smartphone. The world is not getting better and better. It is getting worse and worse and will continue to do so. This will culminate when the Antichrist comes onto the world scene and displays his awesome power and military might at Armageddon. The two world wars and multiple wars of the twentieth century caused this view to be discredited. And since the twenty-first century began with the horrific evil of 9/11, the signs are clear. This century will probably be far more violent and far more oppressive and hostile to Jews and followers of Jesus than the world has ever seen.

3. The *amillennial view* was popularized by Augustine, one of the greatest theologians in the history of the church. He was a brilliant man, but he did what many of the early church fathers did—he spiritualized the text of Revelation and prophecy.

   Augustine said the two resurrections mentioned in Revelation 20:5–6 are symbolic. He thought that the first resurrection symbolizes when a person is born again through faith in Christ. Then the second resurrection describes when Christ comes again and we are given resurrected bodies. I realize Augustine is one of the great theologians in the history of the church, but this is a terrible exegesis of biblical text. The first resurrection describes the resurrection over death, of which Jesus is the first fruit (1 Cor. 15:20). It includes the church when it is raptured. It also includes the martyrs of the faith— those who come to Christ during the Great Tribulation and are martyred for their faith by the rule of the Anti-christ. Bottom line: those in the first resurrection do not have to experience the second death. Our first death is physical. The second death is a spiritual death when the unsaved soul is cast into hell at the final judgment.

4. The *pan-millennial view* is the view I adhered to for many years because of biblical and theological ignorance. This

is the mind-set that because there is so much symbolism in Revelation, nobody really knows what it all means. All we know is that it will all "pan" out in the end. Really, this view is simply the result of biblical and theological laziness. Yes, Revelation and biblical prophecy are difficult to understand. But eschatology, the study of end times, is an important part of our faith. It shows us God's sovereignty over all of history. It gives us urgency in fulfilling Christ's mission in taking the gospel to every people group on earth. And it also helps us view current events and a world increasingly falling into chaos through a biblical lens. Thus, no Scripture passage is more relevant to everyday life than biblical prophecy.

When we read Revelation 19–20, the premillennial view is clearly taught. Combine that with biblical prophecy of the Old and New Testaments, and the evidence is overwhelming. Jesus's second coming will begin His millennial kingdom here on earth. At last, life on earth will be as life is in heaven today. It will be the long-awaited answer to the Lord's Prayer: "Your kingdom come. Your will be done, on earth as it is in heaven" (Matt. 6:10). Jesus's kingdom in heaven perfectly fulfills the will of God. Thankfully, one day His kingdom on earth will do the same. It will be better than we can imagine. You don't want to miss it.

23

The Ultimate Hope

Life on Earth as It Was Always Meant to Be

One reality everyone can agree on is this: things on earth just ain't what they ought to be, whether it is the four million Syrian refugees living in tents because of Syria's civil war or the endemic hatred and evil violence of Islamic terrorists or massive layoffs of good employees in corporate takeovers or an alcoholic husband who beats his wife and children. Whether it is the obscene extravagance of some of the world's wealthy or the horrific poverty of millions in some third-world regimes. Whether it is environmentalists claiming that humans are destroying the earth or environmentalists who hold third-world nations hostage to progress because of their manmade eco-environmental ideology. Whether it's the pandemic of porn addiction of men and boys inside and outside the church or the sexual slavery of many women and girls that enhances their obsessions. Whether it is a man embracing a redefinition of marriage or the hatred of homosexuals. Whether it is bigotry toward certain ethnic groups or the victimization mind-set of so many who are discriminated against. On and on we can go. As we look at the world around us, we know things just ain't like they're supposed to be.

This is why Jesus's second coming is so exciting, for at last life on this planet will finally be as it's supposed to be. In a real sense, it will be like a return to Eden—before man sinned. Jesus will reign and everyone will submit to His reign. The devil and all his temptations to rebel against God will be out of the picture. It will be a time of peace and righteousness and justice like the world has never known since the original sin of Adam and Eve. Biblical prophecy clearly describes it.

Isaiah 9:6–7

We've already looked at this great passage, but we need to study it some more.

Remember, Old Testament prophecy does not distinguish between Jesus's first and second comings. The prophet jumps from Jesus's first coming to His second coming in one verse or from one verse to the next. We go back to Isaiah 9:6–7 to see a clear example of this:

> For a child will be born to us, a son will be given to us; and the government will rest on His shoulders; and His name will be called Wonderful Counselor, Mighty God, Eternal Father, Prince of Peace. There will be no end to the increase of His government or of peace, on the throne of David and over his kingdom, to establish it and to uphold it with justice

and righteousness from then on and forevermore. The zeal of the LORD of hosts will accomplish this.

Remember, the first part of verse 6 refers to Jesus's first coming—His birth and His death. Then the rest of the verse and into verse 7 describe Jesus's millennial reign here on earth after His second coming.

In that time, Christ will rule over all the earth as King of kings and Lord of lords. Yes, there will still be nations with their own leaders, but all will submit to His reign. This also helps us understand why the Antichrist's one-world government will be just another expression of how he is the counterfeit Christ who seeks to usurp Christ in all He does.

Christ, the Perfect Leader

Most of all, this worldwide governance of Christ will be good because of His leadership. He will be known to all as Wonderful Counselor! Can you imagine a president or prime minister of a nation known this way? We go to a counselor when we have an emotional or relational issue we can't resolve on our own. Jesus will be not only King of kings but also a "Good Shepherd" who personally cares for all the people He leads. He will provide perfect wisdom and insight in dealing with everyday issues.

It will also be clear that He is the one and only Mighty God. No more false religions and counterfeit gods. It will be clear who the one true God is. Jesus will be known as that God, and all will see that He is almighty and powerful.

People of the earth will see Jesus as the Eternal Father. We live in a day and age when fatherhood has reached a new low.

More than 40 percent of children born in the United States today are born to unwed moms.[1] Most of these children have no father around. On top of that, many homes have abusive, passive, or absentee dads who may live in the same house but are not engaged in their children's lives. Our world longs for good, strong, loving fathers—fathers of integrity who are dependable. Jesus will be that good father we never lose. He will never forsake us. He will always be with us.

Jesus also will be known as the Prince of Peace. The Antichrist will come into the world as a man of peace, but he will be a fraud. Jesus will be the real deal when it comes to bringing peace on earth. He will give us, humankind, peace with God that leads to inner peace that, in turn, leads us to a desire to be at peace with our fellow human beings.

Micah was a contemporary of the prophet Isaiah. His prophecy of Jesus's millennial reign says, "Then they will hammer their swords into plowshares and their spears into pruning hooks; nation will not lift up sword against nation, and never again will they train for war" (Mic. 4:3b). Oh, how we long for a world like this! The twentieth century had its two world wars, the Korean War, the Vietnam War, and countless others. Now in the twenty-first century, because of the Syrian civil war, more than two hundred thousand Syrian citizens have been killed, and a majority of the four million Syrian refugees are barely existing in tents on the borders of Lebanon, Jordan, and Turkey.[2] And now many more are in Europe.

In the fall of 2014, my wife and I visited some of the Syrian refugees in Lebanon and Jordan. It was heart-wrenching to see their suffering as we shared with them the love of Christ in words and deeds in the distribution of a month's worth of food. When Jesus comes, there will be no more situations like that.

Today Islamic terrorism causes much of the Middle East to be in constant conflict. Muslims killing Christians. Muslims killing Muslims. Civil and tribal wars are realities in Africa, India, and Southeast Asia. On and on it goes. When Jesus comes, that will be history. Oh come, Lord Jesus!

> There will be no end to the increase of His government or of peace. (Isa. 9:7a)

Where Will Christ Reign?

> On the throne of David and over his kingdom. (Isa. 9:7b)

As we've seen, Christ will reign from the throne of David in fulfillment of the prophecy of Samuel concerning the Messiah (2 Sam. 7:12–16). This means He will reign from Jerusalem, the most important city on all the earth. It is the city where Jesus was crucified and buried and rose again. It is the city where He will lead His kingdom here on the earth as He leads in heaven today.

Even though the Jews of Israel and the church will be one when Jesus returns, we must never forget that historically and geographically the biblical story of redemption began *with* Israel and will culminate *in* Israel. We've seen in Zechariah 14:16 how every nation will be sending representatives to Jerusalem each year during the Jewish Feast of Tabernacles (Booths) to pay homage to Jesus. They will come to worship Jesus and be taught by Him. Jesus and Jerusalem will be the center of the world. Micah 4:1–2 describes this special time in the fall of each year in his millennial reign:

221

And it will come about in the last days that the mountain of the house of the LORD will be established as the chief of the mountains. It will be raised above the hills, and the peoples will stream to it. Many nations will come and say, "Come and let us go up to the mountain of the LORD and to the house of the God of Jacob, that He may teach us about His ways and that we may walk in His paths." For from Zion will go forth the law, even the word of the LORD from Jerusalem.

The Character of His Kingdom

Christ's kingdom on earth will be a kingdom of justice. Today we see corruption in government, business, education, and world power structures. We live in a world where people—even "professing" Christians—take advantage of the poor and the weak. Christians, Jews, Muslims, and others are mistreated. This abuse and corruption will end with Jesus's coming, and it will be wonderful. Jesus's government will uphold justice for all. Can you imagine that?

It will be a kingdom of righteousness—no more murder and violence and war on the evening news. No more sexual decadence as the accepted norm. No more double-talk that says what is evil is really good and what God says is good is evil. Because Jesus is righteousness personified, He will make us right with God in how we live on the earth.

Jesus's zealous rule for justice and righteousness will enforce this and see that it becomes a reality on all the earth. The prophet Isaiah writes more about this:

And He will delight in the fear of the LORD, and He will not judge by what His eyes see, nor make a decision by what His ears hear; but with righteousness He will judge the poor, and decide with fairness for the afflicted of the earth; and He will strike the earth with the rod of His mouth, and with the breath of His lips He will slay the wicked. (Isa. 11:3–4)

All Creation Will Be in Harmony

In the beginning of creation, all was in harmony. Adam and Eve had the perfect marriage. They lived in an earthly paradise in Eden. Adam had the perfect job. He got to tend the garden like the greenkeepers do at Augusta National Golf Club. For a quick glimpse that provides some idea of how beautiful Adam made the gardens, watch the Masters Tournament on television every April.

Everything was perfect for Adam and Eve. (This is a reminder that even with a perfect environment, human sin messes up our world. Sociologists, anthropologists, and psychologists who feel that many of the world's problems would be solved if humans were raised in a healthy environment are grossly naive. Yes, a healthy environment helps, but it does not resolve humankind's problems. Adam and Eve had the perfect environment in every way, and they fouled it up with sin.)

Another way the environment was perfect was in humankind's relationship with animals and animals' relationship with other animals. There was no such thing as wild animals. Adam and Eve were vegetarians and so were all animals:

Then God said, "Behold, I have given you every plant yielding seed that is on the surface of all the earth, and every tree which has fruit yielding seed; it shall be food for you; and to every beast of the earth and to every bird of the sky and to every thing that moves on the earth which has life, I have given every green plant for food"; and it was so. God saw all that He had made, and behold, it was very good. And there was evening and there was morning, the sixth day. (Gen. 1:29–31)

There was no killing to eat. Humans and all the animals lived in harmony with one another. The animals began to fear humanity only after humans sinned. When that occurred, there was a shudder within the being of every animal. Instinctively, they knew something wasn't right. Fear was experienced for the first time. And the killing began.

I snicker when I see a show on Discovery Channel or National Geographic Channel that shows wild animals killing other animals for meat. Some naturalists will describe it as "the natural order of things." No, it is not. It is not what God had in mind in creation. It is not what it was in the beginning. Sin began the killing. Human with human. Human with animals. Animals with animals.

When Jesus returns, all of creation will be in harmony:

The wolf will dwell with the lamb, and the leopard will lie down with the young goat, and the calf and the young lion and the fatling together; and a little boy will lead them. Also the cow and the bear will graze, their young will lie down together, and the lion will eat straw like the ox. The nursing child will play by the hole of the cobra, and the weaned child will put his hand on the viper's den. They will not hurt or destroy in all My holy mountain, for the earth will be full of the knowledge of the Lord as the waters cover the sea. Then in that day the nations will resort to the root of Jesse, who will stand as a signal for the peoples; and His resting place will be glorious. (Isa. 11:6–10)

Can you imagine? What an awesome picture!

This is why God's Word tells us there is a groaning in all of creation, a longing for a better world:

> For I consider that the sufferings of this present time are not worthy to be compared with the glory that is to be revealed to us. For the anxious longing of the creation waits eagerly for the revealing of the sons of God. For the creation was subjected to futility, not willingly, but because of Him who subjected it, in hope that the creation itself also will be set free from its slavery to corruption into the freedom of the glory of the children of God. For we know that the whole creation groans and suffers the pains of childbirth together until now. (Rom. 8:18–22)

The world is unsettled and longs for a day when storms will cease, famines will end, natural disasters will be no more, and humans and animals are at last at peace with one another. It really will be like a return to Eden, even though most of humankind will live in a city as opposed to a garden. If you are a follower of Christ, your heart will soar when you read these passages.

This is why Jesus's second coming is the ultimate hope for followers of Jesus. We will reign with Him. We will assist Him in transforming this evil, decadent, and corrupt world into a place of justice, peace, and righteousness. It is a world that people long for today and can only dream of tomorrow. Our worldly governments led by sinful men and women all make a difference for good or bad, but all of them fall short of what we long for. Jesus's government will finally fulfill our dreams—and it will be glorious. This is our ultimate hope! Oh come, Lord Jesus!

Epilogue

Closer than Ever Before

One day in the future all this will come to pass. None of us knows when it will be. When Jesus comes again, there will be rejoicing and celebration for all His followers, yet it will be a time of judgment for all who are not.

If Jesus comes soon, which group will you be in? Celebrating in great joy? Or horrified at your doom?

If you are a follower of Christ, God's Word regarding Jesus's second coming implies some urgency, encouraging us to share with others the good news of Christ so that more and more will be ready for that day.

If you are not a follower of Christ, may you come to your senses and believe that Jesus paid for your sins on the cross and rose from the dead to give us victory over sin and death. May you trust Christ by entrusting your life to Him. May you decide to be a part of Christ's kingdom so that when you pray the Lord's Prayer, "Your kingdom come. Your will

226

be done, on earth as it is in heaven" (Matt. 6:10), you will know that you will be included in Jesus's kingdom.

Salvation from sin and death and the judgment of God comes only one way—through trusting in Jesus Christ as your Savior and Lord:

> Let it be known to all of you and to all the people of Israel, that by the name of Jesus Christ the Nazarene, whom you crucified, whom God raised from the dead—by this name this man stands here before you in good health. He is the STONE WHICH WAS REJECTED by you, THE BUILDERS, but WHICH BECAME THE CHIEF CORNER stone. And there is salvation in no one else; for there is no other name under heaven that has been given among men by which we must be saved. (Acts 4:10–12)

If you are one of those cultural Christians who thinks you are saved because you believe in Jesus with your mind (like the demons of hell), may you, like the demons of hell, be awakened from your spiritual slumber that is really spiritual death.

May your trust be in Him, for Jesus is coming again. His coming again is closer than ever before. Today is the time to be ready!

Acknowledgments

Every time I write a book I'm reminded of what a team effort it is:

Beginning with William Jensen, who helped shepherd this process with Baker Books.

To the editorial staff and team at Baker Books, who provided valuable insight.

To Olivia Mahon, my executive assistant, who spent countless hours typing and researching footnotes and confirming facts and details. As always, there is no way this book would have happened without her. She continues to live out true "extra-mile" ministry.

To Tiffany Buhls, who assisted with research and the typing of the manuscript. Both Olivia and Tiffany serve with a great spirit.

To Danny Akin for his hospitality at Southeastern Baptist Theological Seminary and the use of the school's library in writing a portion of the book.

To Scott and Kim Lamphere and Tom and Susan Goodwin: you know the role you played.

To the members and attenders of Johnson Ferry Baptist Church, who have in worship heard many messages on biblical prophecy that served as a major basis of this book.

And, as always, to my wife, Anne, who shares in ministry with me and offers valuable discernment and discussion about the core message of this book.

Notes

Chapter 1 Birth Pangs

1. "Ancient Jewish History: The Bar-Kokhba Revolt," Jewish Virtual Library, accessed May 17, 2016, https://www.jewishvirtuallibrary.org/jsource/Judaism/revolt1.html.

2. "Shimon Bar-Kokhba," Jewish Virtual Library, accessed June 16, 2016, https://www.jewishvirtuallibrary.org/jsource/biography/Kokhba.html.

3. Vince Albanov, "Rabbi Schneerson or Cult of Personality," *The Examiner*, September 7, 2014, http://www.examiner.com/article/rabbi-schneerson-or-cult-of-personality.

4. Jennie Rothenberg Gritz, "Drinking the Kool-Aid: A Survivor Remembers Jim Jones," *The Atlantic*, November 18, 2011, http://www.theatlantic.com/national/archive/2011/11/drinking-the-kool-aid-a-survivor-remembers-jim-jones/248723/.

5. "Biography: David Koresh," *Frontline*, accessed May 16, 2016, http://www.pbs.org/wgbh/pages/frontline/waco/davidkoresh.html.

6. Sam Howe Verhovek, "Death in Waco: The Overview—Scores Die As Cult Compound Is Set Afire after FBI Sends in Tanks with Tear Gas; Apparent Mass Suicide Ends a 51-Day Standoff in Texas," *New York Times*, April 20, 1993, http://www.nytimes.com/1993/04/20/us/death-waco-overview-scores-die-cult-compound-set-afire-after-fbi-sends-tanks.html?pagewanted=all.

7. Daniel J. Wakin, "Rev. Sun Myung Moon, Self-Proclaimed Messiah Who Built Religious Movement, Dies at 92," *New York Times*, September 2, 2012, http://www.nytimes.com/2012/09/03/world/asia/rev-sun-myung-moon-founder-of-unification-church-dies-at-92.html.

8. "Matayoshi, Mitsuo 'Jesus' Candidate Details," Our Campaigns, February 5, 2010, http://www.ourcampaigns.com/CandidateDetail.html?CandidateID=116421.

9. Sara Malm, "Man Who Thinks He's Jesus . . . Along with Hundreds of Young Women Who Follow Him across the World," DailyMail, January 7, 2014, http://www.dailymail.co.uk/news/article-2535168/Man-thinks-hes-Jesus-hundreds-young-women-follow-world.html.

10. Daniel Rodger and Ryan Turner, "Who Is Pastor Apollo C. Quiboloy?" Christian Apologetics & Research Ministry, accessed May 16, 2016, https://carm.org/apollo-c-quiboloy.